FROM THE PAGES OF THE OFF[

THE BEST OF

INSIDER™

VOLUME 4

TITAN

WWW.TITAN-COMICS.COM

The Best of Star Wars Insider
Volume Four
ISBN: 978-1-78585-1902

Published by Titan
A division of
Titan Publishing Group Ltd.,
144 Southwark Street,
London, SE1 0UP

Collecting material
previously published in
Star Wars Insider magazine.

A CIP catalogue record for this title is available from the British Library.

First Edition October 2016
10 9 8 7 6 5 4 3 2 1

Printed in China.

Editor Jonathan Wilkins
Senior Executive Editor Divinia Fleary
Copy Editor Simon Hugo
Art Director Oz Browne
Senior Designer Andrew Leung
Publishing Manager Darryl Tothill
Publishing Director Chris Teather
Operations Director Leigh Baulch
Executive Director Vivian Cheung
Publisher Nick Landau

Acknowledgments
Titan would like to thank the cast and crews of the *Star Wars*
films, and the animated series: *Star Wars: The Clone Wars* and
Star Wars Rebels. A special thanks also to the teams at Dark Horse
Comics, Marvel Comics, Del Rey, and BioWare for their contributions
to this book. A huge thanks also to Frank Parisi, Brett Rector, and
Micheal Siglain at Lucasfilm for all of their help in putting this
volume together.

THE BEST OF
STAR WARS
INSIDER ™

CONTENTS

006 Daisy Ridley
An interview with Rey from
Star Wars: The Force Awakens

014 Sam Witwer
An interview with the voice of Darth
Maul in *Star Wars: The Clone Wars*

024 *Revenge of the Sith*
The cast celebrate the 10th
anniversary of the movie

034 The Unusual Suspects
The bounty hunters of *Star Wars:
The Clone Wars*

042 Dennis Muren
An interview with the visual
effects master

050 Dark Horse
The history of Dark Horse
Comics' *Star Wars* comic books

070 Searching for the rocket man
A guide to unproduced collectibles

078 Adventures in sound
Ben Burtt and Matthew Wood
discuss sound design in *Star Wars*

086 Knights of the Old Republic
The making of the video game

096 Fangirls flying high
The history of *Star Wars'* thriving
female fanbase

104 The Original Trilogy
Experts, writers, and cast pick out
50 reasons to love Episodes IV, V, VI

118 Hera: a new breed of Hero
An interview with *Star Wars Rebels'*
actress Vanessa Marshall

126 Brian Daley
A profile of the author of the
original Han Solo trilogy of novels

136 Mark Hamill
The man who portrays Luke
Skywalker on his journey
from farmboy to Jedi

146 Tiya Sircar
The actress behind *Star Wars
Rebels'* Sabine Wren interviewed

154 Character Building
Rob Coleman on the digital
effects of *The Phantom Menace*

162 BB-8
The cast of *The Force Awakens*
pays tribute to the saga's latest
droid superstar!

166 Simon Pegg
The actor and longtime *Star Wars*
fan on his *Force Awakens* cameo!

172 Jordan D. White
The editor of Marvel Comic's
Star Wars comic books speaks out

THE RESISTANCE COLLECTORS' COVER
CHOOSE YOUR SIDE: ARE YOU WITH THE FIRST ORDER OR THE RESISTANCE?

STAR WARS
THE FORCE AWAKENS
INSIDER

FEATURING

HARRISON FORD
CARRIE FISHER
ANTHONY DANIELS
PETER MAYHEW
DAISY RIDLEY
OSCAR ISAAC
JOHN BOYEGA
LUPITA NYONG'O
ADAM DRIVER
GWENDOLINE CHRISTIE
DOMHNALL GLEESON
J.J. ABRAMS
AND MORE!

TITAN
ISSUE #162
US $7.99
CAN $9.99
JAN 2016

7 25274 22493 7

REY
DAISY RIDLEY

ISSUE 162
JANUARY 2016

THIS MONTH, FAR, FAR AWAY....

The novelization of *Star Wars: The Force Awakens* released

Star Wars: Darth Vader Volume 2: Shadows and Secrets trade paperback released

Star Wars: I Am a Droid released

Star Wars: I Am a Jedi released

Star Wars: I Am a Pilot released

Star Wars 14: Vader Down, Part V released

Star Wars: Darth Vader 15: Vader Down, Part VI released

Star Wars: Obi-Wan & Anakin, Part I released

If the true story of Daisy Ridley's overnight rise to prominence were a movie, it would be dismissed as too far-fetched. A young actress with assorted bit parts to her name, Ridley made her motion-picture debut in the most eagerly awaited movie of all time. No pressure there, then! Thankfully, she delivers a staggering performance, in a role not only pivotal to *Star Wars: The Force Awakens*, but also to the rest of the new trilogy to follow.

It's safe to say that there has not been a more high-profile movie in which a newcomer makes their debut. Ridley is not just a role model for young female *Star Wars* fans, she is a living example that—with hard work and talent—a dream, no matter how big, can become a reality.**—Jonathan Wilkins**

Daisy Jazz Isobel Ridley (born April 10, 1992) appeared in minor television roles and music videos before being cast as Rey in the Star Wars *sequel trilogy.*

DAISY RIDLEY IS

REY

Clockwise, from top: Rey on Jakku; Daisy Ridley as Rey brandishes her staff; on the run with Finn.

NEWCOMER DAISY RIDLEY MAKES HER DEBUT AS REY, A SCAVENGER ON THE PLANET JAKKU.

Star Wars Insider: How did you first hear about the part of Rey?

Daisy Ridley: The first time I actually heard about this I was with some friends. One is a makeup artist and the other is a stylist. Somebody said, "Did you hear *Star Wars* is coming out?" I immediately emailed my agent, and said that I really needed to be seen for this. I don't know why; I just had this weird feeling. I wound up getting an audition. So, for the first audition I was an hour early. Literally pacing up and down outside. I'd never been

nervous like that before. It was the first time in an audition process that I felt everyone was rooting, not for me, but for the idea of an unknown actor getting the part.

Did you know you were going for the lead?

I knew it was a big part, but I didn't know that it would be the lead. I didn't know what Rey's journey would be and where she would end up. It was only when I read the script that I realized the enormity of things, not only for her, but her place in the whole story.

How did you find out you got the part?

My last audition was really amazing. A few days later, I knew I'd hear from J.J. Abrams, and my phone was broken. I didn't get the call. I didn't know what was going on. I finally got through to him, and he told me I'd be starring in *Star Wars*! I was outside a theater where my friend was in a show, of which I missed the first half while all this was going on. I remember kicking a bottle on the ground like everything had changed. But it was all the same. And then I had to watch the rest of the show. My phone died. I couldn't call anyone. I sat on the Tube [the London Underground] going home not able to tell anyone for an hour! Then,

finally, I told my mum and sister.
But, it didn't really kick in for months.

How did you tell your family?
I burst the front door open and went,
"I got *Star Wars*!" When I told my dad,
who was asleep at the time, he just
swore. That's how it happened.

**How was that time for you, when
you wanted to tell the whole world
and couldn't?**
The time between knowing and the
announcement was so strange. I was
thinking about it as if I were pregnant,
like I couldn't tell anyone until the
three-month mark. It was originally
a month, and it kept extending. My
birthday was really hard. I sat with
all my friends, and it was really hard
not to say anything. As time went on,
it got easier. My mum, dad, and
sister knew, so I had that.

**What does it feel like to star
in a movie that has such
global appeal?**

I'm just starting to realize how big a
thing it is. When J.J. Abrams told me
I got the part, he said that my life was
going to change. I could imagine it,
but I couldn't feel it, until it began to
happen. The people who have done
it before are coming back and it's like
a family. So, I feel honored that I've
been allowed to continue the journey
with my part as well as being part
of the team.

Were you a fan of the franchise?
I remember being in the cinema and
watching one of the films and being
terrified. But because I was younger
than the first generation of *Star Wars*
fans, it wasn't such a huge thing in my
life—until now. But it does permeate
popular culture. It's on magazine
covers. It's referenced everywhere.
But it was only until this year that it
became a really big part of my life.

Who's your favorite character?
Luke Skywalker. I think of it more as a
universal thing. He embodies so much
of everyone. Everyone starts out on
a path; then circumstances change,

make me, that's what I'll bring to the character.

What would you like to impart to young girls on this journey?
I would say, be strong and be thoughtful and take care, and realize how you're affecting other people. Learn and grow and don't be scared if things are offered to you that you're not sure about, but that may change your life. Jump in feet first. Take everything you can and appreciate every day. Appreciate the people around you who support you and never feel on your own, because you never are.

Who is Rey and what is her role in the story?
Rey begins in her own world. She goes on this crazy adventure and meets Finn and BB-8, and she finally starts to make these bonds she's never had.

Can you talk us through your look?
We went through many versions of Rey's hair, and a few versions of her costume. When we finally decided on the hair, and I put the costume on, I could feel everyone react, that's how she should be. Everything is supposed to look like Rey put it together herself. So, the hair is the iconic three buns, which we call the three knobs! The costume is gorgeous. It's pretty, but she works in it. Everything she's got fits her perfectly. I put the costume on and I feel pretty badass.

Talk us through the training process.
I started stunt training just a few weeks after I found out. We did hand-to-hand and used boxing to warm up. J.J. wanted me to look like I work out. So I've been working on the upper body. That was four hours a day, four days a week for three

and things happen, and you go to a new path. The thing that's always with him is the good. He's the good against the evil. He's looking out for Leia and Han Solo too. So, he's got other people's best interests at heart. The choices he makes are positively affecting, not only him, but the people around him as well. I think that's what so many people do in life and that's probably why I feel like that. He's someone I can relate to.

Do you have a favorite line from *Star Wars*?
It's from *The Empire Strikes Back*. Yoda tells Luke that he has to go in a dark cave. Luke asks Yoda, "What's in there?" And Yoda says, "Only what you take with you." That brings everything together; the idea that everything you have inside you

hopefully will lead to good things. Luke, even at the end, hoped for the best in his father, and the best there was. So you have to give it to him that his hope held out.

What are the life lessons that *Star Wars* offers you?
Family is incredibly important, but I also think in 50 years time, I'll look back and really realize the life lessons that I learned from this part of the journey as kind of a whole. So hopefully, I'll learn some more life lessons on the way.

What will you bring to *Star Wars*?
I'm still early on in my life, let alone in my career. But, hopefully, I'll bring freshness and self-confidence, but with vulnerability. All the things that

"REY BEGINS IN HER OWN WORLD. SHE GOES ON THIS CRAZY ADVENTURE AND MEETS FINN AND BB-8, AND FINALLY STARTS TO MAKE BONDS SHE'S NEVER HAD."

LAWRENCE KASDAN
ON DAISY RIDLEY

"We were very fortunate to get Daisy to play Rey because Daisy is an awesome physical specimen, yet at the same time she's a wonderful young actress who is learning all the time. You see this openness in the world, not just to the story she's in, but to acting itself. She's physically very impressive. This is a very demanding part physically. At the same time, she has this incredible beauty and a wit about her that we love from the tradition of British actresses. You feel this is someone who could be in these environments and survive, and that's not easy. These are tough environments and tough situations."

JOHN BOYEGA
ON DAISY RIDLEY

"Daisy Ridley is a hard worker. She's very serious and passionate about this. From the moment I met her, she was fixated on making this role believable and relatable. She's worked hard in collaboration with J.J. Abrams to make Rey loveable and soft, vulnerable, innocent, but at the same time you believe that Rey can become stern, and hard, and kick some butt! She's really strong, and it helps to have someone like that to bounce off of. We're able to collaborate in certain scenes and get the best laughs. It's been amazing not being a young lead by myself. I love the fact that it's a duo of leads. So, whatever experience we go through for the first time, it's both of us going through it. In real life and in the movie. The whole experience, the process, has helped create balance in the galaxy far, far away and on Earth!"

"IT'S JUST SO BIG. THERE ARE MOMENTS WHERE I'M LIKE, 'I'M FLYING THE *MILLENNIUM FALCON!*'"

J.J. ABRAMS ON DAISY RIDLEY

"We looked for a long time at many people. What we were looking for was someone who felt that she was capable of everything. It's a crazy thing, but this character needed to be brought to life by an actor that didn't have limitations. We needed someone who was going to be vulnerable, tough, terrified, thoughtful, sweet, and confused to take on the burden of this role and do it with authenticity. We needed someone who is able to go to this deeply emotional state and do it again and again, in some cases with brand-new actors; in other cases with actors that didn't exist at all, and in other cases, legendary actors. She needed to do all of this, and on top of everything, be an unknown. I didn't want someone who everyone knew who you had seen before.

To find someone no one knew, who could do all these things, took a lot of looking. Luckily we had [our casting directors] Nina Gold, Theo Park, and April Webster in the US working to help us find this person. It was a long search, as it needed to be. We found some great people, but it wasn't until we found Daisy that we thought we'd found the person who can do that sweet, light stuff; she has an incredible smile. She's beautiful. She could do the spirited stuff as well as the tough and emotional.

When she started doing fight training, she had such ferocity. She does this ferocious, gritting-of-her-teeth, primal strength thing. On the one hand she's very relatable and delicate and new and innocent and, at the same time, she's insanely wise. And wildly tough. She's sort of limitless in what she can do. So, when she came in, it was clear we had someone who was going to be enormously special and make a big impact. We realized it had better be in this movie. She's too good to pass up."

months. Without the guys we're training with, there's just no way John Boyega and I would have gotten through Abu Dhabi! The running was so hard. It was a relief when there were explosions, because we needed a break from the running. I haven't stunt trained for a while, but I'm still fitness training to keep the levels up. There are such long days that you need the energy it brings.

What sorts of things do you do?
Stunt-wise, we'll do warm-up and sparring, and kickboxing. Then, I've been climbing. So, I started at a proper climbing wall, and now they have one on the stage. I really like it now. There were days when, if I slipped, my confidence was lost. But I really like it. It's so amazing doing something you haven't done before and feeling that you're gaining knowledge in it.

How was it training to fight with a staff?
We started the staff training with a wooden stick. I don't know how I did it; the adrenaline must have kicked in on the day. I never thought I'd be able to carry on as long as I did doing the fight sequence. The staff was fun. On the day of the fight scene, I was petrified. It was the first action thing I'd done. After the fight, I felt good. I felt like all the training had been for a good reason. In training, you feel like you're pushing yourself to the limit. Then, you get on set and push further. It's an incredible feeling.

What did you get out of the training?
I was really pleased with the training. Rey is an incredibly strong female character. I'd never climbed before; I'd never done fight training before. It's such an amazing feeling to scale a 30-foot wall, or get through a fight with an incredible swordsman. I feel like I held my own, and that's an amazing feeling.

Did you enjoy working in Abu Dhabi?
Abu Dhabi was really nice because we were able to go there a day early. John and I were taken around the mosque and palace, which

ANTHONY DANIELS
ON DAISY RIDLEY

"Daisy is taking on the mantle from the past films. I'm surprised she can breathe. She does more than breathe. I've seen her on set. She has taken to it. I envy that skill and the ease that she appears to have. The effort that goes on behind it is something else, but you don't see that effort. You see her absorb into a film set, absorbing it into her. I'm so admiring of her and John Boyega."

were really lovely. We had a couple of days to get used to the heat as well. It was so hot that you could literally feel the sand burning through your shoes. But, once you give in to the heat, it's OK. You know it's consistent; it's not going to change, so there's no point in fighting it. But everyone was so well looked-after.

When it got to the scenes where we had to run, the hardest part was when it was a mix of hard and soft sand. That was a killer on the legs.

The night before the last day of filming, that run was easier, but my lungs were really pushing it. It got hotter and hotter. You'd go from doing lots of stunt things, then to acting and intimate moments. Towards the end of Abu Dhabi, I looked back and thought, I've really come a long way since the beginning. I could do the first few days again.

How did you feel when you first stepped onto the *Millennium Falcon*?
What was so strange was that the crew was hundreds of people then suddenly it was just a few of us. It's such an iconic set and J.J. really wanted it to be perfect, so there was no mistaking what we're trying to create. It's just so big. There are moments where I'm like, "I'm flying the *Millennium Falcon*!"

How did Rey come to be so mechanically minded?
Rey's always worked with machines. That's what she does and what she knows. When she winds up on the *Falcon*, she's never flown anything like it before. But she's grown up around mechanics, so she uses what she knows to get out of the situation, and start on her journey.

How did you feel about being on set with the legacy cast?
When I first met Harrison Ford, we just sat down for a coffee together. He was talking about his experience in the whole thing, not just Han Solo, but the *Star Wars* saga. Then we all had dinner together, which was great.

Was Chewbacca everything you dreamed of?
It's so funny seeing Chewie up close. He's got a little moustache that is lighter than his face. And, he's just so big!

Is *Star Wars* about family?
Yes, and the family theme translates everywhere. Even on set, it feels like a family. It's that feeling of bonding. Because Rey is trying to find her place in this world in the same way I was trying to find my place in the world, the similarities were really nice. I felt so welcomed and taken in, and people seemed to care how I felt, which translates into the Rey thing as well. She suddenly has these people who care about her.

Do you feel ownership over Rey?
I realized what this film might be to people. I hope that people will love it. I think they will. I feel like I'm working with my film family. Every day is fun. I haven't had one day where I didn't enjoy it. There are moments when I think how many people love *Star Wars*, and it's scary trying to fit into that world that people know so well and love so much. It's nerve-wracking thinking what Rey might represent to these people and whether they'll like her or not.

Was that the most surreal moment?
The first few months of doing the job was so surreal, I can't even remember some of it. I suddenly felt part of the excitement, part of something that people were going to love and people were excited to see again. You feel you're not alone. Everyone is part of this whole thing, trying to make *Star Wars* happen again in the best way. I think people are going to love it.

What is it that you want audiences to take away from the movie?
I'd love for people to feel the way we do working on it. There's such a good feeling about the film and what we're doing and the characters that are being made and formed in front of our eyes. I'd love for the audience to understand each of the characters' stories and connect with the new characters, and I hope that their love for the old characters returns even more than before. I'd love for people to leave the cinema thinking, aside from all the action and the fights, that it's an incredible story of people finding their place in a world. ☺

Clockwise, from top: Flying the *Falcon* with Finn; rescuing BB-8; Rey races across Jakku on her speeder!

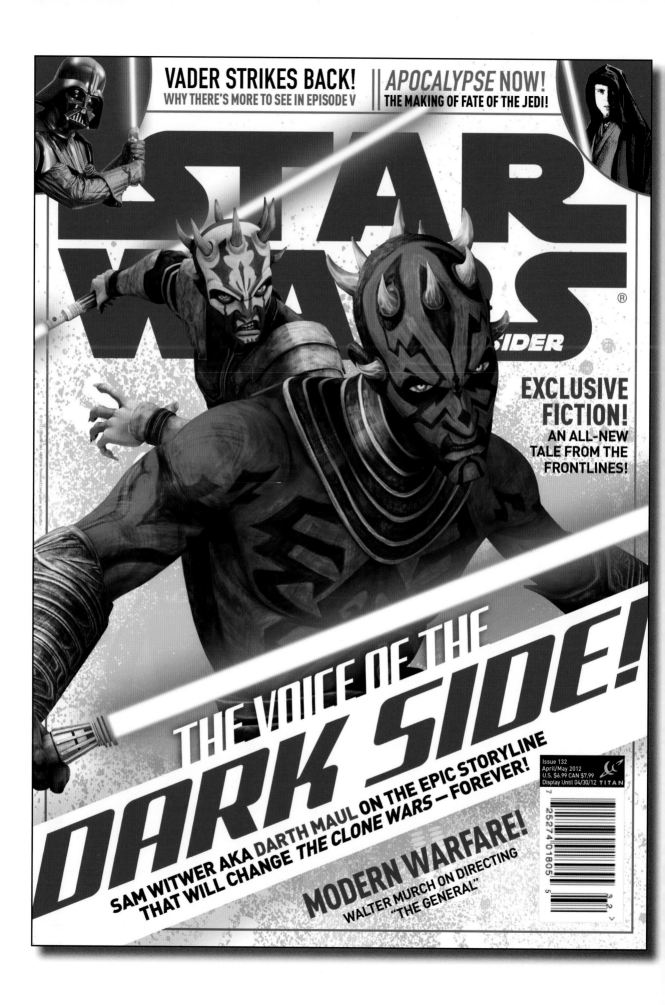

VADER STRIKES BACK!
WHY THERE'S MORE TO SEE IN EPISODE V

APOCALYPSE NOW!
THE MAKING OF FATE OF THE JEDI!

STAR WARS

SIDER

EXCLUSIVE FICTION!
AN ALL-NEW
TALE FROM THE
FRONTLINES!

THE VOICE OF THE DARK SIDE!

SAM WITWER AKA DARTH MAUL ON THE EPIC STORYLINE
THAT WILL CHANGE THE CLONE WARS — FOREVER!

MODERN WARFARE!
WALTER MURCH ON DIRECTING
"THE GENERAL"

Issue 132
April/May 2012
U.S. $6.99 CAN $7.99
Display Until 04/30/12   TITAN

7 25274 01805 5

DARTH MAUL
SAM WITWER

ISSUE 132
APRIL/MAY 2012

THIS MONTH, FAR, FAR AWAY....

Star Wars Activity Handbook 2012 released

Star Wars: The Essential Guide to Warfare released

Kinect *Star Wars* released

Star Wars: The Clone Wars Magazine 11 release

Star Wars: Agent of the Empire: Iron Eclipse, Part 5 released

Star Wars: Knights of the Old Republic: War 4 released

Star Wars: Dawn of the Jedi: Force Storm 3 released

Darth Vader and Son released

Star Wars Identities: The Exhibition opened in Montreal and Edmonton

Star Wars: Scourge released

Star Wars: Blood Ties: Boba Fett is Dead 1 released

Star Wars: Blood Ties: Boba Fett is Dead 2 released

Star Wars: Knight Errant Volume 2: Deluge released

Back in 2008, I was lucky enough to interview a young actor who was starring as the lead character in a groundbreaking video game called *Star Wars*: The Force Unleashed. The actor in question was Sam Witwer, and he was on the cusp of a prestigious career. He soon became a stalwart *Star Wars* performer with three appearances as Darth Vader's secret apprentice over two Force Unleashed games and a guest role in Soul Calibur IV.

His incredible knowledge of *Star Wars* has led to memorable podcast appearances where he dissects and analyzes the saga in satisfying detail. Most significantly he has voiced numerous characters on *Star Wars: The Clone Wars* and *Star Wars Rebels*, including Emperor Palpatine and Darth Maul.—**Jonathan Wilkins**

Samuel Stewart "Sam" Witwer (born October 20, 1977) portrayed Lt. Crashdown in Battlestar Galactica, *Doomsday in* Smallville, *and Aidan Waite in the US/ Canadian version of* Being Human *on Syfy. His* Star Wars *roles include Galen Marek/Starkiller in* Star Wars: The Force Unleashed *and Darth Maul and The Son in* Star Wars: The Clone Wars. *Most recently he has portrayed Emperor Palpatine in* Star Wars Rebels.

BEING BISECTED BY A JEDI AND
PLUNGING DOWN A SEEMINGLY
BOTTOMLESS PIT WOULD
ORDINARILY PROVE FATAL—
BUT NOT FOR DARTH MAUL!
SAM WITWER PLAYS THE
LONG LOST WARRIOR
IN *STAR WARS: THE
CLONE WARS'*
EPIC SEASON
CONCLUSION.

BACK FROM THE DEPTHS!

Star Wars Insider: Before you were cast, what was your opinion of Darth Maul?

Sam Witwer: The thing with Darth Maul is that we all want to know more about him. He shows up and creates this incredible impression—and then he's gone! We've all been clamoring for him to return. The fun thing about these episodes of *Star Wars: The Clone Wars* is that we learn a little bit about what he's been doing for the last 10 years and it's not good. He's been uncomfortable.

What did you think when you found out Darth Maul *was* returning, and that you would be playing the role?

Dave Filoni [executive editor] hinted that he might have something for me after the Mortis episodes [in which Witwer voiced the role of the Son—Ed], and so I was naturally curious. I assumed it was going to be some bounty hunter or something, which I would have been thrilled with. When he informed me that they needed an actor to play Darth Maul,

I just had a geek-stroke and lost the power of speech! Dave not only said that he wanted me to play Darth Maul, but that he wanted to take it in sort of a "Gollum" direction. When I read the script I saw what he meant, but also saw that this might be an opportunity to take it in a "Colonel Kurtz" [from *Apocolyse Now*] direction.

How did this influence the character?
We decided that he might be pitiful one moment and dangerous the next, creating this maelstrom of conflicting emotions and unpleasantness. We all have our opinions about who he is, and that creates expectations, so what do we do? We blow away all expectations and say he's insane! It makes perfect sense. If you're going to be dispatched in the way he was, there must be huge consequences for having him come back. He can't just come back with mechanical legs and say, "I'm the same old Darth Maul that I ever was." There was a major cost, and it's consistent with the other things we see in the movies.

Palpatine says that the dark side of the Force leads to abilities that some would consider to be unnatural, and one of those things is cheating death. The Sith see death as defeat. The Jedi see it as the natural progression of things. The Sith don't look at it that way; they want to control everything. You can't gain any more power if you die, so one of the things that all the Sith do is try to preserve themselves at all cost.

For example Darth Vader is all about that. He gets burned and put in a suit, but that's somehow preferable to death. In a way, Darth Maul has done something similar. He's wallowed in these caves, eating garbage, living in these horrible conditions. Through all his grief and connection with the dark side of the Force, these spider legs made of garbage have grown out of him as manifestations of his pain.

> "HE CAN'T JUST COME BACK WITH MECHANICAL LEGS AND SAY, 'I'M THE SAME OLD DARTH MAUL THAT I EVER WAS.'"

How do you feel about the character now that you've played him?
He's a fearful man. He feels that his rage and hatred have kept him alive, along with his fear of death. He has a twisted sense of humor and he's far more dangerous than people realize. I looked at him as purely muscle: He was the ultimate hitman. But we learn that he's also potentially a general. He's tactically minded, strategically minded, very smart and politically savvy. He was raised by Palpatine—or so we've understood—so he's good at things that you might not expect.

Let's also not forget that Darth Maul perhaps was intended to participate in the Clone Wars. Maybe he was supposed to be General Grievous or even Count Dooku? There was a plan for him, a purpose for him and all of that was stripped away by Obi-Wan.

BROTHERLY LOVE?

Sam Witwer: "It's sad to see how hard Darth Maul works just to get back at Obi-Wan; it's kind of tragic, especially when you take into account Savage and where he sits with all this. Savage is not necessarily a bad guy, or at least didn't start out that way. We can imply from Savage's back-story that Maul had a similar story. We explore that a little bit, too. I think the relationship between Maul and Savage is very interesting as Maul will eventually look upon Savage as his apprentice."

FIRST IMPRESSIONS

Sam Witwer: "I went to a sneak preview of Episode I the day before it opened. After the movie, we noticed that there was a line at a nearby theater for some guy named Ray Park. So we went and met Ray Park. He was a total sweetheart to us and this was just before the film was going to open that night, out there in Skokie, Illinois!

"My first impression of Darth Maul was at once, this brutal, dangerous, terrifying warrior and Ray Park who was just the nicest, coolest guy you could ever meet. I think between those two experiences—seeing the movie and meeting Ray—that this character really has a special place in my heart.

"The next time I met Ray was years later. I wasn't even an actor when I saw first saw Episode I. I met Ray and I tried to explain to him, 'You know, Ray, this is gonna sound weird, but in a videogame, I sort of fight you!' I tried to explain the whole Force Unleashed connection, but I don't know if he understood what I was saying because I was geeking out! Then a week later, we were both signing at a convention and I'm like, 'OK, you see now? I'm sort of a Star Wars character, too!' He's a wonderful guy."

How has he changed?
In the first two episodes, we focus on the madness of what's happened to him, how he's been disabled for a decade, and lost a lot of what he was trained as. The way he speaks is muddled and he's not the same person he once was.

In the next episode—after he is reunited with Savage and gets put back together a little bit—he still doesn't quite know where his place is, but we do get that ultimate dark warrior that we were hoping to see back. We see pretty much exactly what we thought we were going to see: a very angry, very efficient warrior who wants nothing more than to fight Obi-Wan Kenobi.

As the story continues, he realizes that fighting and destroying Obi-Wan ultimately isn't satisfying. He has many opportunities to kill Obi-Wan, but he keeps prolonging it and realizes that this has to last; he's been dreaming about it for 10 years and can't just kill Obi-Wan quickly! He starts developing plans and aspirations, but at the center of those aspirations is, ultimately, revenge against Kenobi.

What was it like to record these episodes with Clancy Brown (Savage Opress) and James Arnold Taylor (Obi-Wan)?
I love the way James plays Obi-Wan! No matter how much you beat that guy up, he'll always have some snarky response; he's like Indiana Jones!

I've been a big fan of Clancy since I was a kid, going back to *Highlander* and *The Shawshank Redemption*. I met him when I was doing the Mortis trilogy last season. He brought his son in because he wanted autographs from the people that were working on *The Clone Wars*, and I had no idea that Clancy was part of the show. I was recording the Mortis episodes and Clancy walks in and says, "Hey, you're the apprentice from The Force Unleashed, will you sign an autograph for my kid?" It was weird—he should have been signing autographs for *me* not the other way around!

"MAUL STARTS DEVELOPING PLANS AND ASPIRATIONS, BUT AT THE CENTER OF THOSE ASPIRATIONS IS REVENGE AGAINST KENOBI!"

Dave Filoni was talking about some sort of story point and how it would relate to The Force Unleashed and Clancy starts piping in about "Well, in The Force Unleashed, this happened..." He really knows his stuff! He's a tremendously well-respected actor and here he is talking to Dave about "my" videogame!

When we were recording, I was so nervous. I think I've settled into it now, but in that first session I felt like the pressure was on. Dave and Clancy were cracking jokes, and I think someone mentioned to me about loosening up and I said, "If I mess this up, millions of fans are going to be mad at me!" Dave Filoni's like, "Welcome to my world, pal. Now read the lines!"

AN AMERICAN SITH?

Sam Witwer: "I know that Darth Maul has an English accent in *The Phantom Menace*, but we didn't worry about that because he's been eating garbage for 10 years and that's going to slightly change the way you talk! But don't worry. We made sure there were moments when he sounds like his old self."

REUNITED WITH VADER AND FRIENDS!

"I had a lot of *Star Wars* toys when I was a kid, but alas, they were either given away or thrown away—or so I thought! My mother recently found my Darth Vader Collector's Case with tons of my old figures. I was stunned. I really thought all that stuff was gone."

Top of this page: Sam Witwer records a scene as the evil Darth Maul for *The Clone Wars*.

Left: Ready for revenge? Darth Maul plots the downfall of Obi-Wan Kenobi.

Right: Can Obi-Wan survive another encounter with his nemesis?

"WHEN WE WERE DEVELOPING STARKILLER, WE THOUGHT OF HIM A[S] AN INTERPRETATIO[N] OF DARTH MAUL, IN PART."

RED MENACE!

George Lucas described Darth Maul as "a figure from your worst nightmare," leading designer Iain McCaig to offer Lucas a design based on a nightmare of his, which although rejected, would later inspire the Nightsisters from *Star Wars: The Clone Wars*.

McCaig's eventual illustration used his own face adorned with markings blending a "flayed flesh face," face-painting of African tribes and Rorschach experimentation [spilling ink onto paper, folding it in half and opening it to produce a pattern—Ed]

Darth Maul's head originally had feathers, which were interpreted by the design team as horns.

THE FUTURE...

Sam Witwer: "Darth Maul will be around for a while in the show. The story takes some really interesting turns, but the psychology of the character is very, very well thought out. It's deep stuff! He's not just a mustache-twirling villain; there's a lot more going on there—there's pain and there's suffering. I don't know how the audience is going to react, but I actually feel sorry for the guy. It'll be interesting if the audience does as well by the time we're done."

You've embodied the dark side before, as the Emperor, Starkiller, and the Son. How is each role different for you?

Those roles are extraordinarily different. When we were developing the character of Starkiller, we thought of him as an interpretation of Darth Maul in part. We created this little geek formula where Starkiller was two parts Han Solo, one part Luke Skywalker, one part Indiana Jones, and one part Darth Maul. Any time that Starkiller was talking to Darth Vader, Darth Maul became the inspiration— I thought he should behave more like Darth Maul did in the film. When Starkiller addresses Lord Vader, he sort of assumes that Sith-like posture and voice. Palpatine has the manipulative edge and a wonderful sense of humor, at least when things are going his way.

Since he'd been trained by Palpatine as his protégé, he would've taken a lot from that guy. So we borrowed heavily from Palpatine for Darth Maul and I think he's a much more dangerous character when you realize how smart he is.

The Son was an arrogant character. I felt Darth Maul had to be extremely arrogant; that starts causing trouble for him later, but you don't necessarily see that at first. It's cool because there's a little bit of connection to the Mortis episodes that the fans will pick up on.

I read a scene in the script where Darth Maul is ranting and raving. I was doing my research, and as soon as I read that Darth Maul was muttering to himself, I found myself wondering, "Well what is he muttering about? What has he told himself in order to keep himself alive?" Part of it is remembering his training, so I started bringing pieces of the Sith Code into the mutterings. There is a thought that the Sith had this code that's a mockery of the Jedi Code. It's things like "Peace is a lie" and "There is only power in strength" and all this great stuff. As I was reading that there was this moment where it said something about "Through victory my chains are broken." Immediately I thought, *Yeah, the chains....*

When I was recording the speech that the Son delivers to Ahsoka before he turns her to the dark side —"The chains are the easy part; it's what goes on in here that's hard"—I was ad-libbing and threw that line in. I love how they feature it; there's this moment when Maul is getting disjointed bits of the Sith Code out, trying to remember his training and then he gets to this point where he recites this line about the chains. It makes his insanity specific in that way.

There are things that he talks about that you'll have to turn up the audio and listen to very carefully. ☪

For more from Sam Witwer and video excerpts from this interview, visit www.StarWars.com

Left: Starkiller from The Force Unleashed and The Force Unleashed II and The Son from Season Three's intriguing "Mortis" story arc.

Below: Witwer in full flow as he delivers a speech as Darth Maul.

WITWER'S WORLD

Sam Witwer was born in 1977, making him the same age as the *Star Wars* saga! He has appeared in individual episodes of numerous television shows as well as playing minor recurring characters in shows such as *Battlestar Galactica*, *Smallville*, *CSI: Crime Scene Investigation*, and *Dexter*. He also played the main protagonist, Galen Marek/Starkiller, in the *Star Wars*: The Force Unleashed videogame and its sequel. He can currently be seen in the US/Canadian remake of the BBC's supernatural drama series *Being Human*.

On the big screen, he has appeared in *Crank*, *The Mist*, and *Gamer*.

His talents also extend to music, and he fronts his own band: The Crashtones! Check them out at www.samwitwer.com

STAR WARS

INSIDER

REVENGE OF THE SITH!

We Celebrate the 10th
Anniversary of Episode III

ISSUE #157
US $7.99
CAN $9.99
MAY/JUNE 2015
DISPLAY UNTIL:
06/09/15

Titan

LORDS OF MISRULE

EXPLORING THE LIGHTER SIDE!

Jeffrey Brown on Finding
Good in Darth Vader!

**The Emperor and Darth Vader
unite in an all-new tale—inside!**

```
0  74808 01805  5          57 >
```

REVENGE OF THE SITH
IN THEIR OWN WORDS

ISSUE 157
MAY/JUNE 2015

One of the alarming things one notices with the passage of time is that anniversaries crop up surprisingly often. We could probably fill each issue of the magazine with anniversary retrospectives. But the beauty of *Star Wars* is that it's not all about looking back.

However, the 10th birthday of *Revenge of the Sith* was one such anniversary we couldn't ignore. How could we resist the opportunity to revisit what was, for quite some time, the final *Star Wars* movie! How things change.
—**Jonathan Wilkins**

THIS MONTH, FAR, FAR AWAY....

Star Wars Rebels: Always Bet on Chopper released

LEGO *Star Wars Character Encyclopedia Updated and Expanded* released

Star Wars: Kanan 2: The Last Padawan, Part II: Flight released

Star Wars: Episode IV *A New Hope* hardcover collection released

Star Wars: Darth Vader 5: Vader, Part V released

Star Wars Legends Epic Collection: The New Republic Volume 1 released

Star Wars 5: Skywalker Strikes, Part V released

Star Wars 6: Skywalker Strikes, Part VI released

Star Wars: Darth Vader 6: Vader, Part VI released

Star Wars: Princess Leia, Part IV released

Star Wars: The Original Marvel Years Volume 2 released

Star Wars: Kanan 3: The Last Padawan, Part III: Pivot released

Star Wars Rebels "The Siege of Lothal" aired on Disney XD

Star Wars Art: A Poster Collection released

Star Wars: Jedi Academy: The Phantom Bully released

EPISODE III

REVENGE OF THE SITH

IN THEIR OWN
WORDS

THE CAST AND CREW OF
EPISODE III CELEBRATE
THE 10TH ANNIVERSARY
OF THE PREQUEL
TRILOGY'S EPIC
FINALE! INTERVIEWS:
MARK NEWBOLD

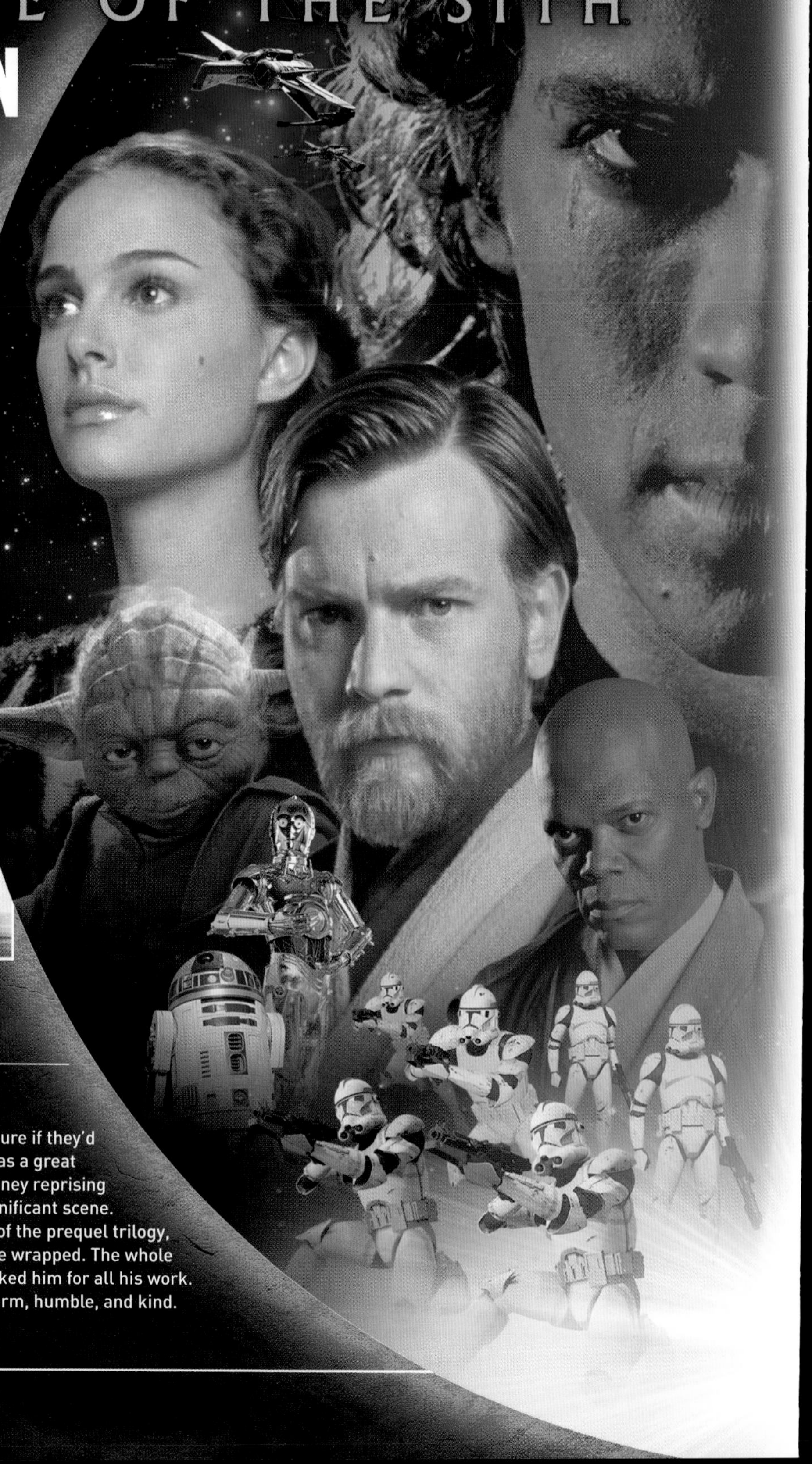

BONNIE PIESSE AS
BERU LARS

**On returning to shoot the final scene for
Revenge of the Sith...**
It was very meaningful for me. I wasn't sure if they'd
invite me back until the last minute. It was a great
surprise to suddenly be on the set in Sydney reprising
the role of Beru, and shooting such a significant scene.
It was Ewan McGregor's very last scene of the prequel trilogy,
so it was a very moving moment when we wrapped. The whole
crew cheered for him and everyone thanked him for all his work.
He seems like a wonderful guy—very warm, humble, and kind.

DAVID ACORD
AS GH-7

On a surprise role...
In early 2004, Matthew
Wood [Grievous and prequel
trilogy supervising sound
editor] and I were working
on restoration and DVD
mixes for the original
trilogy. George Lucas and
the picture editorial crew
were cutting Episode III
at the same time. The rest
of the sound crew hadn't
started yet, but I remember
Matt and I watching this early
cut of it in Matt's office. We
sat down to watch and didn't
say a word for over three hours
–it was a longer version then.
When it was over, I think I just
said, "Wow." We couldn't wait to
get started on it. It would be
another four months before we
would begin sound editorial.
 The GH-7 medical droid, who was
probably just a green tennis ball when
I saw that early cut, was just an
off-screen voice—probably the script
supervisor doing line reads for the actors.
It remained that way for quite a while,
actually. We were doing our final mix at
Skywalker and that reel was coming up. We were
on the mixing stage [Orson Wells Stage "D"] and
George said, "We need an NPR radio voice for the
medical droid." Matthew, knowing that I had been
auditioning for other voice roles, spoke up and suggested
that I try it. Ben Burtt applied some droid modulation to the
performance and we put it up on stage for George the next day.
I was pretty nervous that it would get shot down, so left the stage
before that scene went up. An hour or so later Matthew came by my
office to tell me that George had approved it. Being a part of the
Star Wars filmmaking experience has been a career highlight—but
voicing a *Star Wars* character on screen was fun!

PETER MAYHEW AS CHEWBACCA

On shooting in Australia...
We had a great time in Australia. Chewie is a lot younger in the movie, and therefore I needed a different suit. So I went to costume fittings and got to meet all the other actors there. It was wonderful to meet them and be almost like the grand master!

On working with George Lucas...
George is George—I've known him since the start and he didn't seem that much different. George will stand around, give orders, and things appear. George is very relaxed. When things are going wrong, he will stand there and say, "Hmm, we'll do it this way, we'll do it that way."

ANTHONY DANIELS AS C-3PO

On hitting his marks...
On Episode III, rather sweetly, they gave me different kinds of marks on the floor. Sometimes it was tape, or a bean bag. But this time they gave me these fairly flat things, but in gold. They thought I should have gold marks. That's a nice souvenir. I could feel them a little through my feet!

RICK MCCALLUM (PRODUCER)

On why Episode III is his favorite...
It's the most adult. But I knew back in 1991 there was going to be a major storm over Episode I and II. George knew it. He said, "I know I'm going to lose a lot of my hardcore fan base, but this is the story that I want to tell—it's the saga of a family and it has to start somewhere."

I think anybody who was over 25 years old wanted to see Episode III as Episode I. But George wanted a whole new generation to follow the saga.

I think Episode III brought peace to the two galaxies: the older fans and the younger fans. There are some scenes in there, I think in the last 25 minutes, that are as good as we could have ever done. From the moment Anakin and Obi-Wan are having their fight and Anakin's legs are cut off, it's perfect.

JEREMY BULLOCH AS CAPTAIN COLTON

On returning to the saga...
I was on holiday in Tuscany in 2004 with my family and our cell phone rang. My wife answered it and an American voice said, "Can I speak to Jeremy?" She asked who was calling and he said, "It's Rick. Rick McCallum!"

My immediate thoughts were that this was one of my chums having a laugh! It's not every day you get a famous producer calling you when you are halfway up a mountain. When I got over the shock, he asked me if I was available to cameo as the pilot [of the Alderaan cruiser].

When I arrived at the studio, it was great to meet Ewan McGregor and Jimmy Smits, who played Bail Organa. I also caught up with many of the technicians whom I had worked with some years ago. It was also great to see George Lucas once again, who would be directing my scene. Whilst I was actually filming I had no idea of what my name would be, and it came as a nice surprise that I was to be called Captain Jeremoch Colton, a portmanteau of my name.

It was an honor to be called back, and to be part of the *Star Wars* saga again.

HOWIE WEED (DIGITAL MODELER, ILM)

On his work on Episode III...
I was asked to work on a sequence that was perhaps the most daunting on the entire production: the moment where Yoda takes on the Emperor in a lightsaber duel.

When I first took a look at the sequence, there wasn't much of Yoda with his lightsaber choreographed just yet. That was a huge challenge for Rob Coleman and his animation team. Taking the concept of a very small character like Yoda becoming a total badass was tricky.

For my part in this, I created a digital sub-chamber set that is revealed with a massive mechanical metal iris overhead, where Yoda and the Emperor could finally confront each other. The metal leaves of the iris would open during the fight to reveal the Senate chambers above.

I recall thinking, *How is any of this going to work? It's Kermit the Frog versus the Emperor in full-on black robes, towering over him!*

Coleman and his team really pulled it off. The way Yoda would ricochet from place to place, out-pacing the Emperor, was a whole new style of fighting. The audience really got behind Yoda being a parkour master. This was yet another master stroke from George Lucas. He has a knack for trying new things and making them work.

CHRISTIAN J. SIMPSON (STAND-IN FOR HAYDEN CHRISTENSEN)

On working with Ian McDiarmid...
Ian was absolutely wonderful. It was quite a shock when, on my first day on *Revenge of the Sith*, Hayden was arriving late from makeup and so I had to act out the scene with Ian. He began in his classic Emperor's chair, facing away from me. All I could see was the top of his head and the back of the chair. Then he got the direction to turn around and "face Anakin," which I am delighted to say was me—for that moment!

On keeping an on-set journal...
On set I wasn't "being" the fan; I couldn't,

I was being the professional. But in my accounts I have to speak what was going on inside my head. I know many people on set were also hiding their true excitement of being there, but it spilled over. Even Hayden was so excited to have gotten the part; he still had his moments! We would share little comments, like on the last day of filming, I was proud to be reading Ian McDiarmid's lines for him so Anakin could react. I turned to Hayden and said, "So this is it then —last day," and he looked somber as he agreed, "Yep. Last day." Then I heard George muttering something about the last day as he adjusted a lighting rig! Everyone knew we were working on something special. There was a grand air of history in the making.

KENNY BAKER
AS R2-D2

On a memorable moment on set...
Just seeing the set again on board Princess Leia's ship (the *Tantive IV*) brought back all the memories. Who would have thought, when we were filming the original movie, that some 25 years later we would all be back to the same point, bringing the story full circle? I'm so proud to have been involved in real movie history.

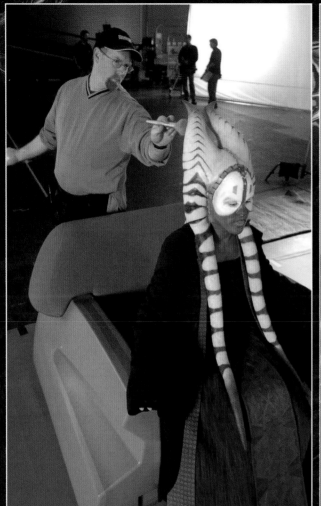

DANNY WAGNER (MODELMAKER AND MAKEUP ARTIST FOR INDUSTRIAL LIGHT & MAGIC)

On his best work...
I would pick the environment maquettes I did for Kashyyyk in [George Lucas' production company] JAK Films' art department. Every Friday, George would arrive to discuss the art and maquettes to give feedback. It was so amazing to be there, contributing my ideas with George and [Industrial Light & Magic concept designer and concept art director] Erik Tiemens and Ryan Church; coming up with new and really interesting worlds. I was pleasing George so much I was receiving "Fabulouso" stamps on my maquettes all the time! I learned that was a rarity. Most people got the work stamped with an "OK." For a while people called me "Mr. Fabulouso."

On meeting a special guest...
I was lucky enough to be a part of the JAK art department when it was announced that George was going to bring in a guest director so he could add some creative input on the film and work with the crew on *Sith*. We all were guessing which one would it be. I was hoping it was Steven Spielberg—and it was!

The meeting went very well and Steven was very open and nice. He was telling us about a helicopter ride he took over a volcano in Hawaii and he had to pay the pilot a lot of money to fly as close as he could to get the best reference he could. This was for Mustafar.

On turning George Lucas into Baron Papanoida...
I was told that something came up in production that concerns George Lucas. I'm thinking, *Oh dear*. "What's up?" I asked. I was told that George was going to have a first-time cameo in this movie and would have makeup on his face and they wanted me to do it. I said, "Oh man! Are you serious? Yes!"

George came in with his daughter Katie who I was also going to makeup for the film. It was nice not having George's entourage, because he was so down to earth and approachable, making jokes and laughing. I applied Katie's makeup first, which was a big help because she told me her Dad doesn't like anything poked on his face, especially his eyes! Her makeup only took an hour. George was next. He came in and sat down.

I explained that I was going to do an airbrush technique with the pressure at 15 to 20 pounds. I thought that would be more soothing than brushing or stippling. He was pretty adamant about his beard not being covered up. After painting him blue, I had to highlight the beard because it changed the color of his normal hair. For his tribal markings, I had a laser-cut stencil made for the design. It was pretty simple: two yellow lines on both of his cheeks and three on his forehead. I did give him highlights and shadow for his face, and eyelid makeup. This was the only time George ever had makeup on his face, and I did it! When I was done, he stood up and looked straight in the mirror and said, "Good job. I like it."

ON YOUR TRAIL!
CREATING THE BOUNTY HUNTERS

ROMANCING A JEDI!
SATINE'S STORY REVEALED

STAR WARS

INSIDER

ISSUE #117
MAY/JUNE 2010
U.S. $5.99 CAN $6.99

THE RETURN OF
BOBA FETT
READY FOR REVENGE!

THE UNUSUAL SUSPECTS
STAR WARS: THE CLONE WARS

ISSUE 117
MAY/JUNE 2010

Dave Filoni is a great gift to an interviewer. One small question can elicit a lengthy, articulate response that is rich in detail and very well reasoned.

For this piece, we wanted to showcase some of the cool bounty hunters that were to be introduced in *The Clone Wars*. Dave presents an expert guide to the whys, hows, and wherefores of these characters. *Star Wars: The Clone Wars* and *Star Wars Rebels* are both team efforts with talented folk from a variety of departments pulling together. Without a leader as inspirational and passionate as Dave, I doubt the results would be anywhere near as impressive.—**Jonathan Wilkins**

Dave Filoni (born June 7, 1974) is best-known for his work on Avatar: The Last Airbender *and* Star Wars: The Clone Wars. *He is also an executive producer on the series* Star Wars Rebels.

THIS MONTH, FAR, FAR AWAY....

Star Wars: Head-to-Head released

Star Wars Rebels: Join the Rebels released

Star Wars: A Scanimation Book released

Star Wars: The Clone Wars: Bounty Hunter: Boba Fett released

Family Guy: Something, Something, Something, Dark Side aired

Star Wars: Fate of the Jedi: Allies released

Star Wars: Legacy 48: Extremes, Part 1 released

Star Wars: Invasion: Rescues 1 released

Al Williamson dies, age 79

Star Wars: The Clone Wars: In Service of the Republic trade paperback released

Star Wars: Knights of the Old Republic Volume 9: Demon released

Star Wars: The Clone Wars Character Encyclopedia released

Star Wars: Dark Times 17: Blue Harvest, Part 5 released

Star Wars: Invasion: Rescues 2 released

Star Wars: Legacy 49: Extremes, Part 2 released

Star Wars: Legacy Volume 9: Monster released

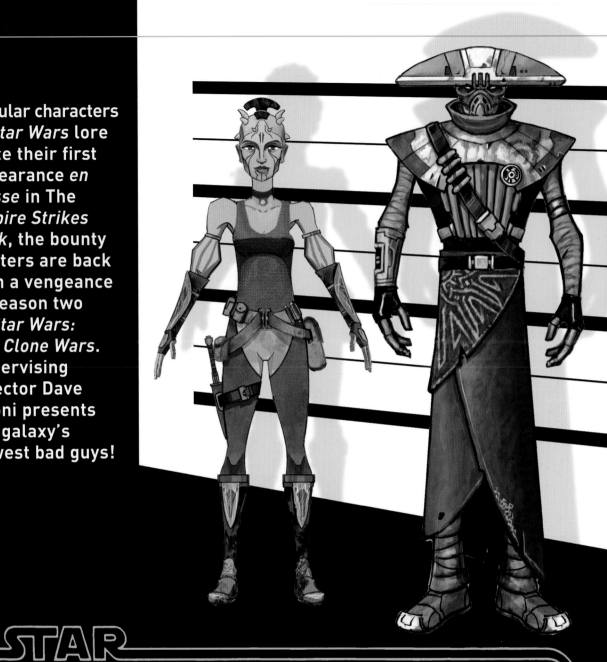

Popular characters of *Star Wars* lore since their first appearance *en masse* in The *Empire Strikes Back*, the bounty hunters are back with a vengeance in season two of *Star Wars: The Clone Wars*. Supervising director Dave Filoni presents the galaxy's newest bad guys!

STAR

THE UNUSUAL SUSPECTS

WARS™

BOUNTY BUNCH

"When it came to the bounty hunters, we really wanted them to have a lot of colorful elements to their costumes along with different little knives and bits of gear like all the details you see on Boba Fett's outfit. It's great that over the years the fans have decided, 'Oh, those are sonic wrenches,' and other details," says Dave Filoni. "It might have just been a piece of metal that was shoved in the pocket for effect! We try to make our bounty hunters interesting like that. They definitely have more logos; for some reason there always seems to be a slight NASCAR-effect to the bounty hunters when you see all these emblems. I think that comes from Boba Fett being yellow-shouldered with green armor, and then later having red gauntlets. It makes them stand out. You know instantly they're not Republic or Separatists.

"It's fun to pay off that season-opening promise of 'Rise of the Bounty Hunters', because here come a whole bunch of them!"

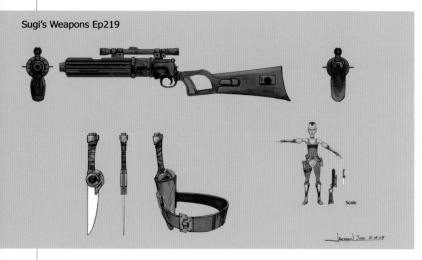

Sugi has dark skin tone

Sugi is same species as EethKoth

SUGI

All Sugi/Sugi weapon illustrations by Jackson Sze.

"She is a Zabrak [the same species as Darth Maul]. We mainly used Eeth Koth as an inspiration for her. There was some debate on whether or not she should have horns. We wondered, do female Zabraks have horns? But let's face it, she's a lot cooler if she has horns than if she doesn't! So since it was never defined, we decided to give her horns. We had a certain way we wanted her shoulders to puff out with a kind of red striping, so there's a little bit of a pirate element to her, with a very specific hairstyle. She really lends herself to being a visually exciting character, but still very human-looking. She turned out to be someone with a really fun attitude. I love the scenes where she's talking with Obi-Wan Kenobi. She seems to stand toe-to-toe with him really well as another very independent, well-spoken being... and she's great with a blaster!"

Sugi Ep219

Sugi production art complete with annotations.

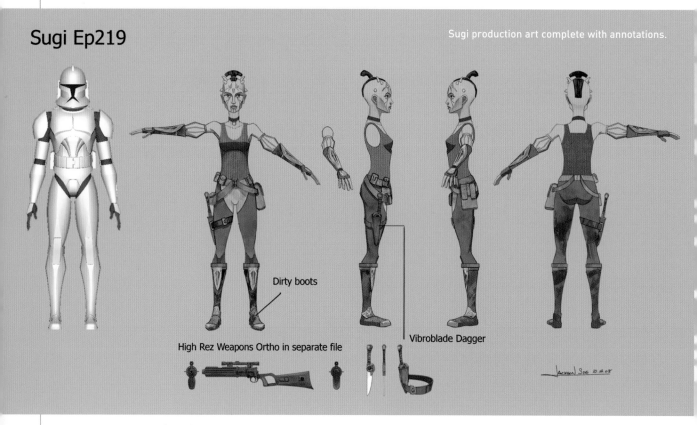

Dirty boots

High Rez Weapons Ortho in separate file

Vibroblade Dagger

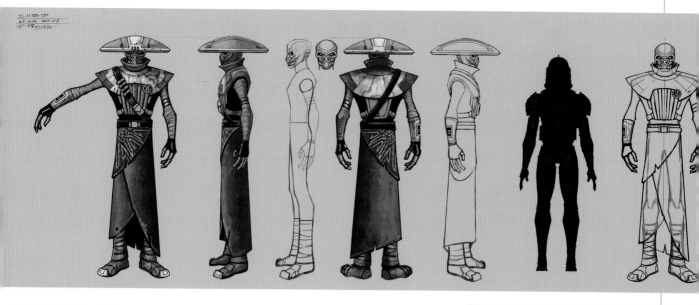

EMBO
All Embo and Embo weapon illustrations by Pat Presley.

"Embo was a design handed to us by George Lucas from earlier concept work. We just modified him a bit. He became a favorite character with the team at Lucasfilm Animation. I don't know what it is, maybe it's that hat, but something about him just connected. Steward Lee [the director], and I really wanted to expand what Embo did, as far as action, to show how skilled these bounty hunters are with their weaponry.

"Design-wise, there wasn't a lot to develop, because we had such a good head-start from George, but we decided that we wouldn't let him speak English. We just went full-out with an alien tongue that we invented. We don't often do full alien speaking characters in *The Clone Wars*, mainly because of the amount of subtitling that would require— and that's a disappointment. But here we had characters reacting to what Embo says, like they do to R2-D2."

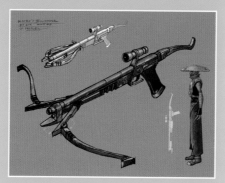

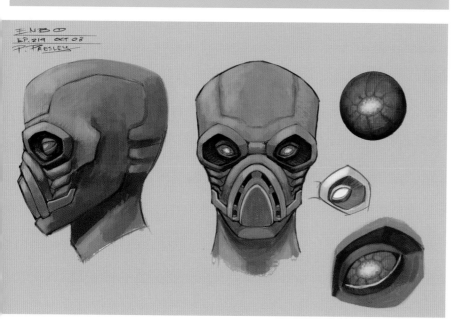

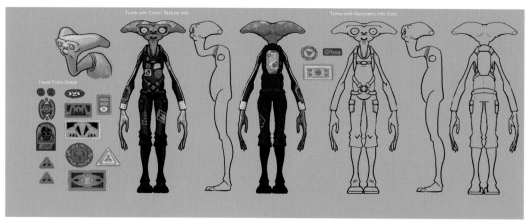

SERIPAS

"This was another design that came to us from George. He is basically a big suit of armor and George wanted this little guy inside him. Wayne Lo [the design artist] did this breakdown for him, which is the exploded view drawing of Seripas that just looks like a Japanese toy. I loved the way it would open up. We wanted to have a lot of little colored lights and stuff inside so we could really see these lights on his face when he's inside the big suit of armor.

"He turned out very cool, but he had a much more expanded role at one point that we had to cut down for time. We have these cool bounty hunters and some of them don't get to do a lot. Once I saw him without the armor on, I wanted him to have a lot of patches on his flight suit. And one of the patches I asked Wayne to include is the *Star Wars* fanclub patch of Darth Vader. So if you look closely, you'll see this little patch that looks a little bit like a Vader helmet. It's that one that he's wearing on his uniform!"

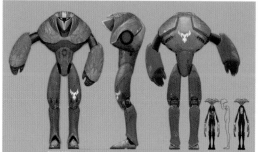

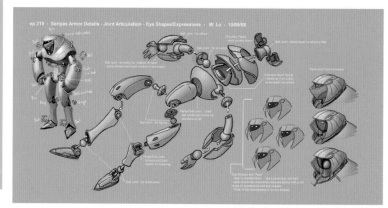

All Seripas images by Wayne Lo

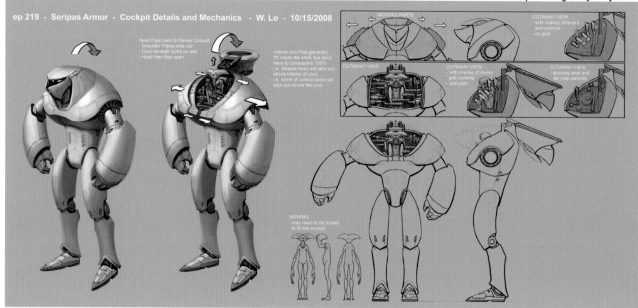

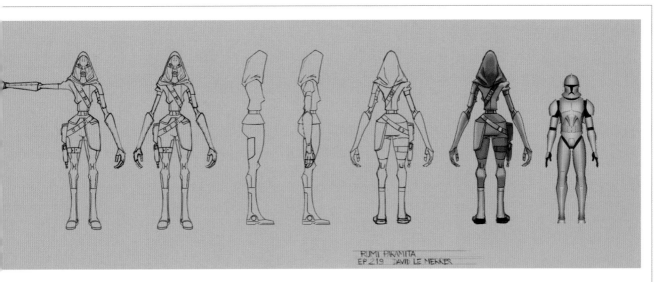

RUMI PARAMITA
EP 219 DAVID LE MERRER

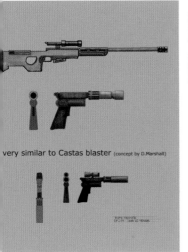

very similar to Castas blaster (concept by D.Marshall)

RUMI PARAMITA

"George will often send us a design and say, 'I want it to look something like this.' Then we have to take it and bring it into *The Clone Wars* world, and sometimes it changes a lot and sometimes it doesn't. But we had a great start with Rumi. She started as a very small mouse, very narrow, which guided how we were going to have the voice-acting done. She's just a very bizarre, classic type of alien, with a large head and thin limbs."

All Rumi and Rumi weapon images by David Le Merrer

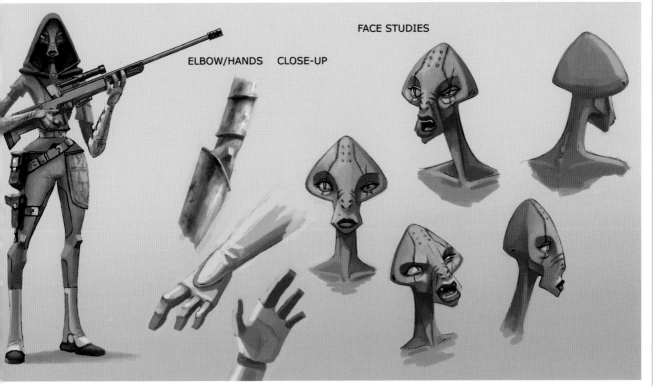

FACE STUDIES

ELBOW/HANDS   CLOSE-UP

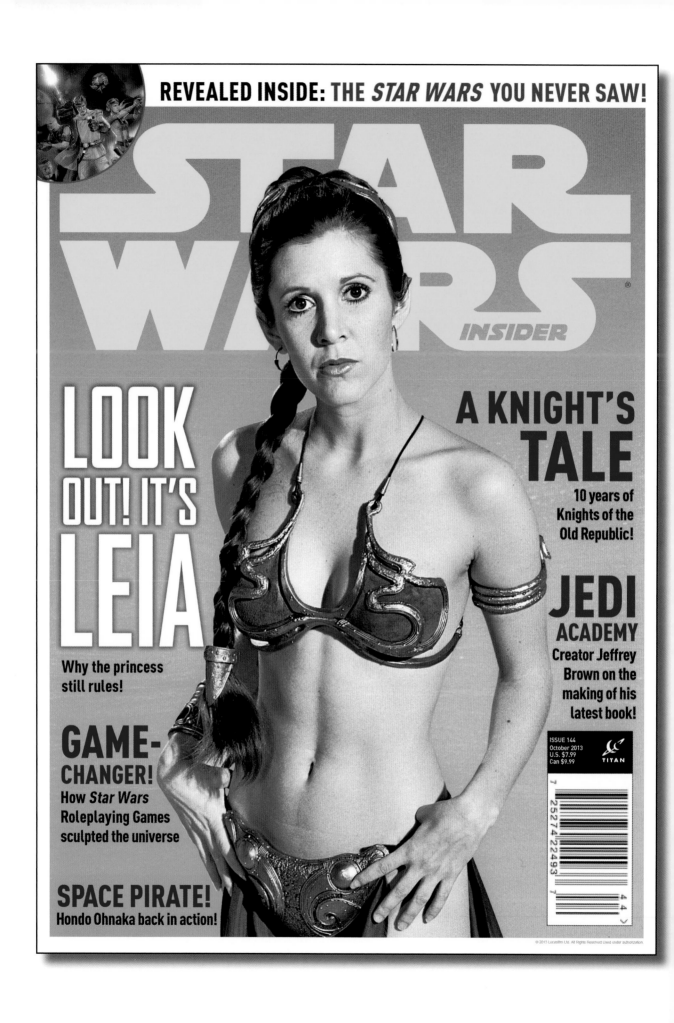

REVEALED INSIDE: THE *STAR WARS* YOU NEVER SAW!

STAR WARS
INSIDER

LOOK OUT! IT'S LEIA

Why the princess still rules!

GAME-CHANGER!
How *Star Wars* Roleplaying Games sculpted the universe

SPACE PIRATE!
Hondo Ohnaka back in action!

A KNIGHT'S TALE
10 years of Knights of the Old Republic!

JEDI ACADEMY
Creator Jeffrey Brown on the making of his latest book!

ISSUE 144
October 2013
U.S. $7.99
Can $9.99

TITAN

DENNIS MUREN
VISUAL EFFECTS

ISSUE 144
OCTOBER 2013

THIS MONTH, FAR, FAR AWAY....

The Making of Return of the Jedi released

The Star Wars 2 released

Star Wars 10 released

Star Wars: Ewoks: Shadows of Endor released

Star Wars: The Clone Wars: The Complete Season Five released

Dennis Muren has been a fixture of the *Star Wars* universe since the very early days. A huge talent in his field, this interview came to us courtesy of former Industrial Light & Magic general manager Thomas G. Smith. Smith wrote one of the earliest books on the company: the seminal *Industrial Light & Magic: The Art of Special Effects*. While some of this interview appeared in the book, this is a complete version of Smith's discussion—transcribed from the original tapes—with a true master of his craft.—**Jonathan Wilkins**

Dennis Muren, ASC (born November 1, 1946) is a visual effects artist and supervisor. He is best known for his work with Steven Spielberg, James Cameron, and George Lucas. To date, he has won eight Academy Awards for Best Visual Effects.

DENNIS MUREN
EFFECTS VISIONARY

DENNIS MUREN WAS ONE THE VISUAL EFFECTS MASTERMINDS ON THE ORIGINAL *STAR WARS* TRILOGY, AND HAS WORKED ON MANY SUBSEQUENT ILM MOVIES. ALONG THE WAY, HE'S WON EIGHT OSCARS FOR VISUAL EFFECTS AND EARNED HIMSELF A STAR ON HOLLYWOOD'S WALK OF FAME. HERE, WE PRESENT A CLASSIC INTERVIEW CONDUCTED BY FORMER ILM MANAGER (1980 TO 1985) THOMAS G. SMITH FOR HIS 1986 DEL REY/ BALLANTINE BOOK *INDUSTRIAL LIGHT & MAGIC: THE ART OF SPECIAL EFFECTS*.

How did you get started in visual effects?
This goes back to when I was very young— probably six or seven years old. I was fascinated by the spectacle and the possibility of movies. I was eight or nine before I realized they were actually made by people and that what I saw wasn't really there. That was exciting! I got a movie camera a couple years after that. It was literally a $10 camera, an 8mm movie camera. It only had one lens, but it could shoot stop-motion. At first, to see what I shot, I only had a film viewer with cranks to run the film, but eventually I got a projector. But even before that, I was playing with slides, by putting two slides together or scraping on them to see two images superimposed. Then, when I was about 14 years old, my folks bought me a $130 camera. That was a big deal. That camera had reflex viewing [viewing through the lens]. Those kinds of things are important for a kid if you get them at the right age. I shot an awful lot of stuff with that camera and my friends helped me. We did perspective stuff with foreground sets that looked big in the frame. I did some rear projection stuff around that time also. I spent a lot of time reading books from the library in Glendale and Pasadena [California], so I was

accumulating reading material. *Monster* magazine was a big thing for all of us at that age, and through that magazine I met people like Dave Allen and Jim Danforth [now established visual effects artists]. You have to get a peer group and grow with it.

How did you come to know them?
They advertised in the magazine and I wrote to them. So I got to know a lot of these kids and they were in some of my movies and I was in theirs. We used still photographs and we put a sign in front of the house; we called it something like "The Movie Science

Fiction Exposition." By then, Danforth was doing animation for feature films —he's seven or eight years older than me. Growing up with people like Danforth and Allen I learned not to accept things how they are, but to see if there's another way of doing it.

When did you make your film *Equinox*?
That was done the first year of college. I guess I was about 17 or 18. Dave Allen helped us out and he consulted on it.

Did you take a class in cinema?
I wasn't interested in film classes. I didn't like people judging or grading my work.

What was your major in in college?
Business and advertising. I hated business, but my folks said they wanted me to take the classes. I was interested in advertising because I worked on commercials occasionally at Cascade [an advertising production studio in Los Angeles]. I only had classes two or three times a week, and the rest of the time I'd go into Hollywood and see people.

What happened to *Equinox*?
The version we did was about 71 minutes, and I sold it. The whole thing ended up costing about $8,000. I put in about $6,000 and we found an investor so we could add sound.

Did you get your money back?
Almost. I'm short maybe $1,000, which is fine with me. I wanted to complete that project, get it over with and get on to something else. It got a real release, played in a theater. You know, for kids to see their movie in a theater, that's a really big thing!

Where did you work after you left school and before you were working on *Star Wars*?
I worked at Cascade with Phil Kellison, a real pioneer in visual effects. Cascade was the effects house that did the Pillsbury Doughboy. There was no effects work around in the early '70s. It was really grim. I was out of work for about two years, trying to get another film project going with [special effects artist] Jon Berg. I went and visited [*Silent Running* director] Doug Trumbull and he didn't have any work, but [motion-capture pioneer] John Dykstra was there. That was the first time I met John.

I tried to get into Disney and there wasn't any work there. Very frustrating! I was just about ready to get out of the business—I was going to go into medicine or something [laughs]. I never would have, but I was seriously thinking of leaving film. Then Phil left Cascade, so Cascade hired me back, full time as their cameraman. This also allowed me to get into the cameraman's union. I had always wanted to get into the union, but

Top: Dennis Muren.

Main image:
Muren lines up Vader's TIE fighter for its attack run during the making of *Star Wars* (1977)!

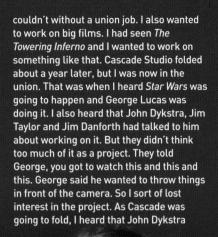

couldn't without a union job. I also wanted to work on big films. I had seen *The Towering Inferno* and I wanted to work on something like that. Cascade Studio folded about a year later, but I was now in the union. That was when I heard *Star Wars* was going to happen and George Lucas was doing it. I also heard that John Dykstra, Jim Taylor and Jim Danforth had talked to him about working on it. But they didn't think too much of it as a project. They told George, you got to watch this and this and this. George said he wanted to throw things in front of the camera. So I sort of lost interest in the project. As Cascade was going to fold, I heard that John Dykstra

finally got the *Star Wars* job. So I called him up. He liked the idea that I had done stop-motion. He was planning on motion control and thought there was a correlation; both are "non-real-time" thinking and he liked that I had done that. He still hadn't hired [effects photographer] Richard Edlund at that time.

So about that time, John called me back and said he wanted me to work on *Star Wars*. There were two groups at that time: Doug Trumbull's group and John Dykstra's. I didn't know anyone in the Trumbull group.

Could you tell that *Star Wars* was going to be something special?
Most people felt it would be a little picture. It would do OK and that was about it. The one guy, the only guy, who thought this was going to be something really big was the ILM unit driver. The guy who ran the errands. He said this is going to be a monster hit. Everybody else, including me, liked the genre but thought it would just be a little movie. The script was really good. One of the best scripts I had ever read. But I thought, *How can they do something like this?* It seemed really bizarre.

When was the first time you saw a cut of *Star Wars*?
I saw one reel, the last reel. But when I saw my own stuff, it wasn't the same. I didn't see *Star Wars* as a movie. Films I've worked on are movies but they aren't "real" movies to me. Even when a film is done, I have trouble seeing it as others will. I see shots and think about the shooting. I see how they changed it from what I expected. They are plastic. When I was a kid and saw a film, it was like they were made in stone.

What goes through your mind when you're doing miniature photography?
Well, it starts out with the storyboard. The snow walker scene is a good example. You could do that five ways, but you have to realize there has to be a way for the animators to get in and manipulate the model each frame to animate it. In order to make that practical, you've got to make modifications here and there. And the final step is the lighting, which can also change the whole thing. You've got to know how it should look. I've spent years of my life

"THERE ARE SHOTS IN *STAR WARS* THAT HAVE NEVER BEEN DONE BEFORE. I'D SNEAK THEM IN AND TRY THEM OUT."

observing how these things look—you know, the reflections off things and how bright the reflections are. I look at real things; for example, Where I live in Marin, I try to figure out how the fog happens to look the way it does. You don't want to shoot these things in smoke, because smoke is a problem with stop motion. The smoke will move around and not stay the same frame to frame. It is a matter of light and haze. And so we put up a bridal veil to make it look like atmosphere. This is an old stage trick and it works!

You were involved in the development of go-motion: 'the process where a model is moved during exposure, creating a blur, and where the movements are controlled with motorized rods attached to the object and programmed with a computer'. Tell me about that.
We attempted go-motion on *Empire*. We used motion control for the major moves of the tauntaun. We had talked for years about this; Phil [Tippet, head of ILM animation on *Empire*], Jim Danforth and me. We talked about how blurs help stop-motion. So we blurred the major movements of the tauntaun with motion control, but it still wasn't enough to my satisfaction. So when we did *Dragonslayer* (1981), Phil was talking about stop motion for the dragon and I said, "Stop-motion is jerky. Why don't we try motorized rod puppets?" So we decided to try to program it, but we needed more memory on the computer because there were so many channels for all the rods. We modified an Apple computer for the moves, and then it was a learning process for Phil to learn how to do his own programming. It was time-consuming.

Isn't it possible to take the jerkiness out of the animation?
Jim Danforth did some great stop-motion for

When Dinosaurs Ruled the Earth (1970) in the traditional way. But as far as I know, Danforth was the only one who could do it.

I heard Phil Tippett say it is not the blur as much as it is the lack of mistakes.
That is 99 percent of it. The blur helps but isn't everything. We actually shot a test of the dragon walking two ways: one without the blurs and one with the blurs. You could barely see the difference. The same thing goes for spaceships. It is more the dial-up speeds and the slow-down speeds. Let's just say with normal stop motion that every three frames you are slightly off. That is eight times a second that you are off. And that's doing incredibly well; doing 100 things without making a mistake. With go-motion you can go back, repeat it, and correct it.

So if you had to choose one of your works till now to be your best, would *Dragonslayer* be your favorite?
It is like choosing a child. *Dragonslayer* was the most challenging and successful in some ways. But I've got little scenes here and there that are amazing. There are shots in *Star Wars* that had never been done before. I'd sneak them in and try them out.

Can you remember an example in *Star Wars*?
When you're following along with a spaceship, I wanted one that looked like it was a hand-held shot with the camera not steady. I didn't ask to do it. I didn't want to have to convince anybody to do it, so I just did it. I made it look like it was hand-held; I programmed the stars to move the way they should. It wasn't any harder; I had to program the stars anyway. It worked very well and later we did it quite a lot. In *Jedi*, there is a lot of it and the look is astonishing. That is the best capability of the motion control stuff. It allows essentially one person

47

> "I LIKE SCENES WHERE THERE'S SOME SMOKE AND YOU CAN ALMOST SEE IT AND THEN IT CLEARS A LITTLE AND YOU CAN SEE SOME MORE."

to assemble a collage of shots and make it come out and look like one thing. You couldn't do it if you had to deal with a crew on a set.

Which shots from *The Empire Strikes Back* are you particularly fond of?
To me, the asteroid sequence, I really like that. That's one of my favorites.

What else would you like to have on your sample reel?
Well, we have the bike chase from *Return of the Jedi*. On those films you need something like that, some special and memorable scene. For me the bike chase is the highlight of the film.

What about something from *Indiana Jones and the Temple of Doom*?
I really liked the mine car chase; Mike [McAlister] shot it and did an excellent job in figuring out all the details on it.

But you had a lot of influence in allowing him to use the unsteady Nikon still camera rather than a traditional movie camera. I can't imagine many supervisors who would allow such a low-tech departure!
Yeah, but if I didn't think it was going to work, if I felt Mike couldn't pull it off, I wouldn't have allowed it to be used. If you know your crew real well, you can figure ways to do it and they'll come through. I learned this watching Doug Trumbull. Doug would go on the set and set up the shot then go away. That gave

him objectivity in the screening room. If you don't know the problems, it is easier to tell the crew to do it over again. You don't think, *if I say that, then I've got to do this and that all over again*. It works great for Doug, but it is frustrating for me because I want to be out there, doing it.

What's your feeling about the emerging digital technology that is coming along?
Well, first they have to get more memory. When they get enough memory I think it is going to be great.

What do you see yourself doing in the future? Would you direct another movie?
I got that out of me with my first film, *Equinox*. The need to express something in me was in that film. As far as a lot of people seeing my work, I had that with *Star Wars*. So I'm in an odd position of not knowing! At times, I sort of don't want to do it much more. Then someone will come up with a scene and I'll say, "Hey, there's another way we could do this." I'll make it look all documentary or all backlit or something. It hasn't been done, or done as cheaply. I've seen an awful lot of people who have broken away from visual effects and who have never had the success they had again. I don't want to go through that—I think of all my struggling years.

I'm pretty thankful for what's here, with the environment of ILM. You know they are here to work and work; I couldn't do it on my own. People come up with things I couldn't have thought of. If I tried producing or writing I might not be very good at it and it would be a serious mistake to make.

You've worked with Steven Spielberg and George Lucas. How would you compare the two?
It's a hard question to answer. Steven depends on feedback from people he works with, perhaps to a greater extent than George. But on the other hand, when we discussed the bike chase in *Jedi* and I was making suggestions, George just said, "Go ahead and just do it." Steven has never done that. George went back and redid a lot of it, but we had our chance. When I come up with an idea, George will be thinking about what it is going to cost to do it. He knows a lot about effects. While Steven may just say, "Do it," and he'll face what it costs later... I've learned so much from George and from Steven.

What do you think about when you go to design a shot?
There are so many variables—you can't pull a list out and say, "Well, the camera should move... and it should be at this speed and backlit..." I get into the mood of asking

at what point is this in the fi
fit with the environment? It
instinct. I work on it till it ju

The worst thing is to see
You remember in the 1950s
films were lit so you could s
That's the worst thing. I like
there's some smoke and yo
see it and then it clears a li
can see some more. Now yo
something like *The Godfath*
Cotton Club (1984) or *The Bl*
(1979) and you just fall over
that. And we did it in the mi
Indiana Jones. Look at one o
mine chase with the car sha
shot. With a shot just a few
you're thinking, *What's wror*
I can't see what's happening.
you put the whole thing all
works in context. That's th
I like. ☺

MARK HAMILL LOSES THE FORCE!

FIRST STRIKE! EMPIRE STORYBOARDS

DARTH STEWIE

TALKS SITH!

STAR WARS
INSIDER

THE
OLD REPUBLIC

A MORE CIVILIZED AGE?

THE CLONE WARS
DAVE FILONI ON THE
SECOND SEASON

STAR WARS INSIDER #114
January/February 2010
U.S. $5.99 CAN $6.99

FALSE FETT?
STAR WARS'
**WEIRDEST
SIDESTEPS
UNEARTHED!**

DARK HORSE
A COMIC BOOK LEGACY

ISSUE 114
JANUARY/FEBRUARY 2010

Dark Horse Comics' impressive run of *Star Wars* titles provided readers with a monthly fix of *Star Wars* for 23 years from 1991-2015. Boasting storytelling styles both innovative and traditional, Dark Horse's titles ranged from sprawling epics to short stories, and from tales that made us cry to ones that made us laugh. In short, there was something for every *Star Wars* fan, all told with style by some of the industry's finest writers and artists. Of course, *Star Wars* comics continue at their new home, Marvel, but let's not forget how Dark Horse kept the flame burning as brightly as it ever could.—**Jonathan Wilkins**

Dark Horse Comics was founded in 1986. The company's first Star Wars *series was the acclaimed* Dark Empire *in 1991. During the period in which they held the license, Dark Horse republished the Marvel* Star Wars *comics and released several compilations of works, in the* Star Wars Omnibus *series. The Omnibus imprint also showcased Marvel's* Indiana Jones *series. The company released titles from a wide variety of periods of* Star Wars *history, both prior to, and following, the events of the movies.*

THIS MONTH, FAR, FAR AWAY....

Star Wars: The Clone Wars "Grievous Intrigue," "The Deserter," "Lightsaber Lost," "The Mandalore Plot," "The Duchess of Mandalore," and "Voyage of Temptation" aired on Cartoon Network

Star Wars: Rebel Force: Trapped released

Star Wars: Heroes released

Star Wars: The Clone Wars 12: Hero of the Confederacy, Part 3 released

Star Wars: The Clone Wars: Day One released

Star Wars: Knights of the Old Republic Volume 8: Destroyer released

Star Wars: Galaxy of Intrigue released

Star Wars: Dark Times 15: Blue Harvest, Part 3 released

Star Wars: Knights of the Old Republic 49: Demon, Part 3 released

Star Wars: Crosscurrent released

Star Wars: Legacy 44: Monster, Part 2 released

DARK HORSE RISING

∷∷∷∷∷∷∷∷

DANIEL WALLACE DISCOVERS HOW DARK HORSE COMICS REINVIGORATED THE *STAR WARS* SAGA!

"We wanted to create sequels to the movies we loved," says Mike Richardson, the comics fan and entrepreneur who challenged publishing giants Marvel and DC in 1986 when he founded Dark Horse Comics—one of the most successful independent publishers in the industry. Though it was Marvel who first got the ball rolling on *Star Wars* comics in the 1970s and 1980s, Dark Horse revitalized the license in the early 1990s and proved it could do as good if not better a job than either of the "Big Two."

"The *Star Wars* comics that came before us tended to look like other comic books," explains Richardson. "They were line art with a four-color process and an inker putting in the black outline. It looked very traditional. They also had giant rabbits with ray guns. That, for me, didn't really suit the *Star Wars* universe that well. [At Dark Horse] we wanted to make it very cinematic and as close to the films as possible."

One of the challenges at Marvel was that they had their own universe to worry about. Over the decades, Marvel had built up an interconnected superhero setting populated by such characters as Spider-Man, Captain America, and the Hulk. By necessity, *Star Wars* took a secondary role, but Richardson vowed to make it the centerpiece of his company's portfolio if he could bring the license to Dark Horse. "I knew the potential that *Star Wars* had and I knew that Marvel wasn't realizing it," he says. The proof that Dark Horse could do it came by developing other popular sci-fi movies into hit comics in the late 1980s.

"We wanted to achieve higher sales than the new character launches we were doing, and thought we could do it by taking movies and creating sequels to them," he says. "It was a shortcut to creating established characters, because it takes years to build up a Superman or a Spider-Man." Up until that point, comics based on movies tended to be straight adaptations, or received only a fraction of company attention, which limited their potential. "At the time nobody cared about comics based on movies."

THE "WOOKEES", THEY TOOK OVER AN
X-WING TO ESCAPE PURSUING IMPERIAL FORCES? THE FIRST

Richardson worked with 20th Century Fox to secure the comics rights to the *Aliens* franchise, and put out a six-issue *Aliens* miniseries in 1988. It was a monster hit. "We went through six printings and sold hundreds of thousands of copies, and did it in a way that wasn't normally done at that time—a six-issue series that really was the next movie."

With *Aliens* in Dark Horse's stable, Richardson next acquired the rights to *Predator*, another major property from 20th Century Fox. Richardson and Dark Horse staffers started brainstorming sequel ideas immediately after a screening of the film. "We walked out of the theater and said, 'What about the Predator in the steel jungle, on the hottest day of the year?'" he says. The *Predator* comic once again continued the story rather than adapting it.

"We had problems with getting the likeness rights to Arnold Schwarzenegger, so we put his character in the hospital with radiation sickness and picked it up with somebody else in the city," says Richardson.

After racking up further success with *Aliens vs. Predator* (14 years before the movie franchise did the same thing), Richardson and Dark Horse turned their full attention to *Star Wars*.

"I'm a *Star Wars* geek from the old days," he says. "When I was in college, we used to sit around and say, 'What do you want to do tonight? Let's go see *Star Wars*!' I saw it 19 times in the theaters, and I considered it the crown jewel of all licensed properties." Richardson contacted Lucy Wilson in Lucasfilm's new publishing division and made an impassioned pitch for the then-dormant comics license.

"I told her how we would do it differently than Marvel," he recalls. "It would have a different look and be very cinematic. It would be the sequel to *Return of the Jedi*. Lucy had seen a proposal at Marvel that had gone nowhere, attached to [writer] Tom Veitch and [artist] Cam Kennedy. I immediately contacted both of them and we started discussing a comic-book sequel to the movies called *Dark Empire*."

AS LEIA GRIPS THE CONTROLS OF THE *BLASTER CANNON*, SHE REMEMBERS THE WORDS OF HER *TEACHER...* LETTING HER MIND MERGE WITH THE *LIVING ENERGY FIELD* THAT BINDS THE GALAXY TOGETHER--

LUKE IS RIGHT...

I CAN FEEL THE *FORCE* MOVING THROUGH ME... GUIDING MY *HANDS* IN THE TERRIBLE TASKS OF WAR--

LEIA ORGANA, WIFE OF HAN SOLO, ALREADY A MOTHER OF TWO, IS, ABOVE ALL THINGS, A *JEDI WARRIOR!*

GOT HIM!

THE DARK HORSE YEARS

The early years of Dark Horse shaped the Legends and produced some of the best spin-off stories of all time. Here's the easiest ways to get your hands on these tales:

Dark Empire (1991-1992)
The landmark six-issue series is widely available as a trade paperback, and also appears in the hardcover collection *Luke Skywalker: Last Hope for the Galaxy.*

Classic Star Wars (1992-1994)
The Al Williamson stories (issues #1-20) have been collected in three trade paperbacks: *Classic Star Wars: In Deadly Pursuit, Classic Star Wars: The Rebel Storm,* and *Classic Star Wars: Escape to Hoth.* Also available are *Classic Star Wars: The Early Adventures* (written and illustrated by Russ Manning), and *Classic Star Wars: Han Solo at Stars' End* (featuring an adaptation of the Brian Daley novel with art by Alfredo Alcala).

Tales of the Jedi, The Golden Age of the Sith, Fall of the Sith Empire (1993-1997)
The initial 1993 series, published as *Tales of the Jedi,* is collected in the 400-page *Star Wars Omnibus: Tales of the Jedi Volume 1* as Ulic Qel-Droma and the Beast Wars of Onderon and The Saga of Nomi Sunrider. Also included are both of the "Sith Empire" series.

Dark Empire II (1994-1995)
The six-issue series has been collected in trade paperback form, but seek out the trade paperback's second edition—it includes the two-issue wrap-up *Empire's End.*

Star Wars: Droids (1994-1997)
Star Wars Omnibus: Droids collects the entire series in one 440-page volume, including the storylines The Kalarba Adventures, Rebellion, Season of Revolt, and The Protocol Offensive, as well as the rare "Artoo's Day Out."

Tales of the Jedi: The Freedon Nadd Uprising, Dark Lords of the Sith, The Sith War, Redemption (1994-1998)
The rise and fall of Exar Kun is told in these tales, all of them reprinted in the 464-page *Star Wars Omnibus: Tales of the Jedi Volume 2.*

River of Chaos (1995)
This four-issue Princess Leia miniseries went uncollected for years until its recent inclusion in *Star Wars Omnibus: Early Victories.* This 336-page volume also includes the stories Vader's Quest, Splinter of the Mind's Eye, Shadow Stalker, and Tales from Mos Eisley.

Heir to the Empire, Dark Force Rising, The Last Command (1995-1998)
These adaptations of Timothy Zahn's trilogy of Thrawn novels are individually available as trade paperbacks, and have recently been compiled in a single hardcover volume on sale this December.

X-Wing Rogue Squadron (1995-1998)
The entire series is available in three separate omnibus editions (each between 300-360 pages), sold as *Star Wars Omnibus: X-Wing Rogue Squadron* Volumes 1-3.

Richardson's acquisition of the *Dark Empire* project helped tip the scales in his favor, and before he knew it Dark Horse was officially the *Star Wars* comics publisher. *Dark Empire* would be the company's first release.

"Cam Kennedy was the perfect artist for *Dark Empire,*" says Richardson. "He had spectacular painted scenes of the ships, characters, and action. It was gorgeous, like watching a Technicolor film of the movie frames. And Tom wrote a story that took place right after the third movie that had Luke fall into the spell of the dark side. In the end, *Dark Empire* was the most successful series we'd ever done."

A sequel to *Dark Empire* with the same creative team soon found its place in the planning cycle. At the same time, Dark Horse began exploring other ways to push *Star Wars* boundaries. This took them far outside the movies—4,000 years outside!

"We were very interested in stories focusing on the past of the Jedi and not the same characters," says Richardson. "Moving out of the Luke Skywalker time period felt like it needed to be a separate series, and clearly labeled so people didn't get confused." That became *Tales of the Jedi,* a series set during the heyday of the Old Republic when the Jedi Knights numbered in the tens of thousands and the galactic frontier ran wild with danger. *Tales of the Jedi* soon became its own mini-franchise, spawning sequels and spin-offs (*Dark Lords of the Sith, The Freedon Nadd Uprising, Fall of the Sith Empire*) and eventually paving the way for projects from other licensees set during the same era, including the 2005 video game Knights of the Old Republic and the upcoming MMORPG, The Old Republic.

By the mid-1990s, Dark Horse had become the most prominent player in the *Star Wars* Expanded Universe next to book publisher Bantam. Richardson, who saw cross-promotional opportunities, secured the rights to the comics adaptations of Bantam's bestselling *Star Wars* novels *Heir to the Empire*, *Dark Force Rising*, and *The Last Command* by Timothy Zahn. All three were strong sellers, prompting Richardson to look toward the novels as potential talent pools.

"We went after some of the authors who had done *Star Wars* novels," he says, including Michael Stackpole, writer of Bantam's *X-Wing* series. Stackpole's novels combined intense space dogfights with the big-cast camaraderie of a starfighter squadron, something that had the potential to translate well into the comics medium. *X-Wing Rogue Squadron*, written by Stackpole, debuted in 1995 and enjoyed a 35-issue run.

"We thought *X-Wing* would be a great military title," says Richardson. It was one more element in Dark Horse's plan to diversify its *Star Wars* line, or as Richardson puts it, "to create different tones and different elements."

One of those elements had first appeared in the *Star Wars* Expanded Universe during the time of the classic trilogy. From 1979-1984, *The Los Angeles Times Syndicate* distributed a daily *Star Wars* newspaper strip throughout the U.S. and Canada. The strips had long been out of print when Dark Horse made arrangements to collect and reprint the portion of the run illustrated by the legendary Al Williamson (see *Star Wars Insider* issue 112).

GREETINGS, SOLO.

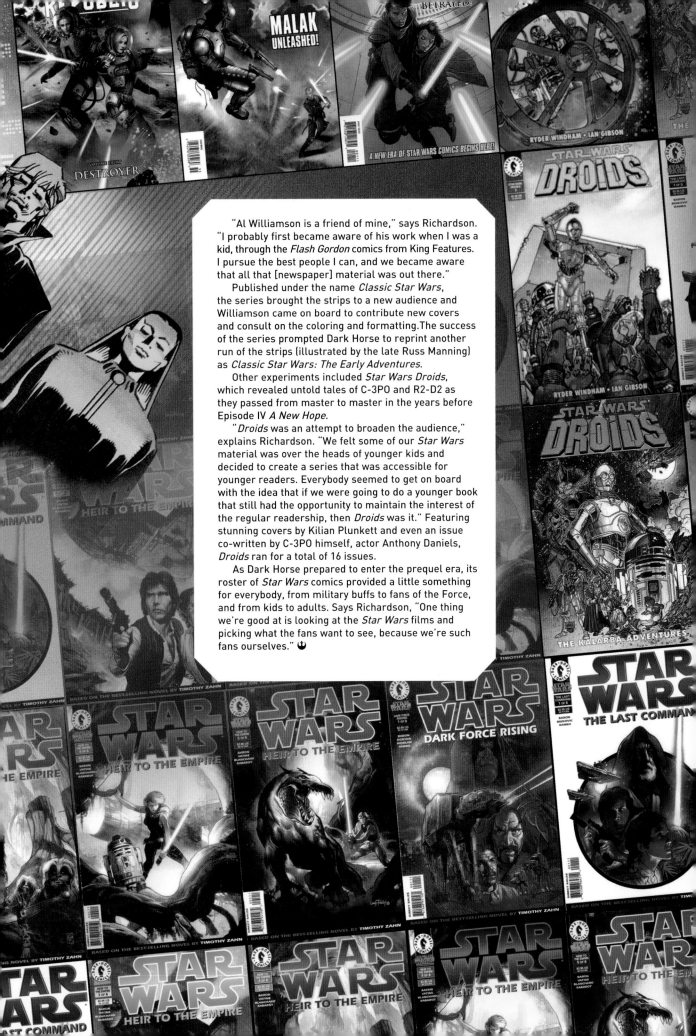

"Al Williamson is a friend of mine," says Richardson. "I probably first became aware of his work when I was a kid, through the *Flash Gordon* comics from King Features. I pursue the best people I can, and we became aware that all that [newspaper] material was out there."

Published under the name *Classic Star Wars*, the series brought the strips to a new audience and Williamson came on board to contribute new covers and consult on the coloring and formatting. The success of the series prompted Dark Horse to reprint another run of the strips (illustrated by the late Russ Manning) as *Classic Star Wars: The Early Adventures*.

Other experiments included *Star Wars Droids*, which revealed untold tales of C-3PO and R2-D2 as they passed from master to master in the years before Episode IV *A New Hope*.

"*Droids* was an attempt to broaden the audience," explains Richardson. "We felt some of our *Star Wars* material was over the heads of younger kids and decided to create a series that was accessible for younger readers. Everybody seemed to get on board with the idea that if we were going to do a younger book that still had the opportunity to maintain the interest of the regular readership, then *Droids* was it." Featuring stunning covers by Kilian Plunkett and even an issue co-written by C-3PO himself, actor Anthony Daniels, *Droids* ran for a total of 16 issues.

As Dark Horse prepared to enter the prequel era, its roster of *Star Wars* comics provided a little something for everybody, from military buffs to fans of the Force, and from kids to adults. Says Richardson, "One thing we're good at is looking at the *Star Wars* films and picking what the fans want to see, because we're such fans ourselves." ✪

DARK HORSE: Phase Two

DAN WALLACE UNCOVERS WHAT HAPPENED WHEN THE PREQUELS HIT MOVIE SCREENS AND *STAR WARS* POPULARITY REACHED FEVER PITCH!

The hype was inescapable. Fueled by the record-setting release of the *Star Wars* Trilogy Special Editions and a tantalizing string of trailers, teases, and sneak peeks for *Star Wars*: Episode I *The Phantom Menace*, 1999 was shaping up to be the biggest year that *Star Wars* had ever seen.

Dark Horse Comics stood ready to ride the wave. After relaunching *Star Wars* licensed comics with *Dark Empire* in the early 1990s, the company had enjoyed a succession of hits that took the saga from the timeframe of the classic trilogy to the vanished splendor of the Republic's golden age. The prequels represented a second phase in Dark Horse's *Star Wars* output—for the first time, the company would be producing work alongside new George Lucas movies that promised new characters, new conflicts, and a fresh sensibility.

Ironically, the massive public interest in the prequels didn't help Dark Horse much during the period from 1999-2005. There simply seemed to be an overabundance of options for fans wanting

to scratch a *Star Wars* itch. "When *The Phantom Menace* was released we experienced an almost immediate drop-off in sales," says Dark Horse's Randy Stradley. "Sales stayed at that lower level pretty much across the board until after the release of *Revenge of the Sith*. During the period of the prequels there was so much *Star Wars* material available that fans couldn't afford it all and were forced to make choices. After the third film, as the product wave subsided, our sales went back up to previous levels."

Stradley notes that the decrease and rebound weren't merely confined to prequel-themed titles, nor was the phenomenon a reflection on the quality and craftsmanship of the era's stories. "I really think it was a case of fan appetite for all things *Star Wars* being temporarily sated," he says.

Dark Horse's prequel era actually began at the end of 1998, with the publication of the first installment of the story arc "Prelude to Rebellion." The event represented two important milestones: The inauguration of a new ongoing series (simply called *Star Wars*, in the vein of the Marvel series that ran from 1977-1986), and the introduction of Episode I's Jedi character Ki-Adi-Mundi.

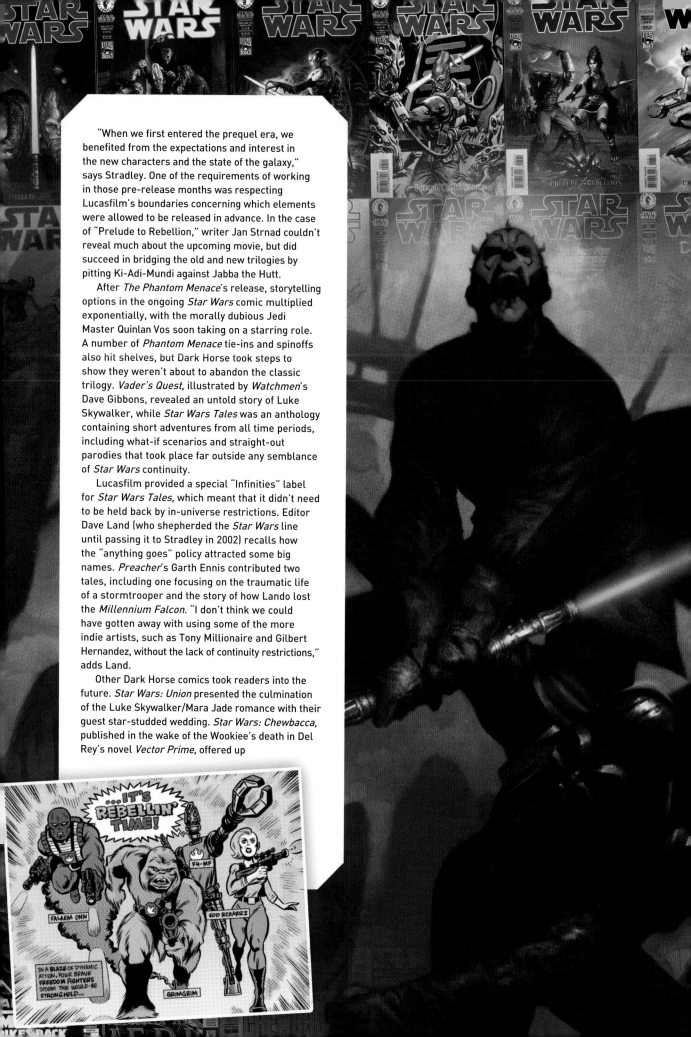

"When we first entered the prequel era, we benefited from the expectations and interest in the new characters and the state of the galaxy," says Stradley. One of the requirements of working in those pre-release months was respecting Lucasfilm's boundaries concerning which elements were allowed to be released in advance. In the case of "Prelude to Rebellion," writer Jan Strnad couldn't reveal much about the upcoming movie, but did succeed in bridging the old and new trilogies by pitting Ki-Adi-Mundi against Jabba the Hutt.

After *The Phantom Menace*'s release, storytelling options in the ongoing *Star Wars* comic multiplied exponentially, with the morally dubious Jedi Master Quinlan Vos soon taking on a starring role. A number of *Phantom Menace* tie-ins and spinoffs also hit shelves, but Dark Horse took steps to show they weren't about to abandon the classic trilogy. *Vader's Quest*, illustrated by *Watchmen*'s Dave Gibbons, revealed an untold story of Luke Skywalker, while *Star Wars Tales* was an anthology containing short adventures from all time periods, including what-if scenarios and straight-out parodies that took place far outside any semblance of *Star Wars* continuity.

Lucasfilm provided a special "Infinities" label for *Star Wars Tales*, which meant that it didn't need to be held back by in-universe restrictions. Editor Dave Land (who shepherded the *Star Wars* line until passing it to Stradley in 2002) recalls how the "anything goes" policy attracted some big names. *Preacher*'s Garth Ennis contributed two tales, including one focusing on the traumatic life of a stormtrooper and the story of how Lando lost the *Millennium Falcon*. "I don't think we could have gotten away with using some of the more indie artists, such as Tony Millionaire and Gilbert Hernandez, without the lack of continuity restrictions," adds Land.

Other Dark Horse comics took readers into the future. *Star Wars: Union* presented the culmination of the Luke Skywalker/Mara Jade romance with their guest star-studded wedding. *Star Wars: Chewbacca*, published in the wake of the Wookiee's death in Del Rey's novel *Vector Prime*, offered up

THE DARK HORSE YEARS

Dark Horse's prequel-era output was prolific, but don't give up. Presented here is a top-line guide to getting your hands on all these stories, which span multiple eras of the *Star Wars* timeline.

Star Wars: Republic (1998-2006)

The prequel era at Dark Horse began with the launch of this series, originally titled simply *Star Wars*. Its early years are notable for the adventures featuring the Jedi Quinlan Vos and Aayla Secura. The series received a name change to *Star Wars: Republic* with issue #46 and began chronicling the events of the Clone Wars, ending its run with issue #83. It has been collected in 18 trade paperbacks, with "Prelude to Rebellion" the first volume in the run. Collectors take note: The 10th through 18th collections are labeled "Clone Wars" volumes 1-9 (and don't carry any outward *Star Wars: Republic* identification).

Vader's Quest (1999)

Darth Vader hunts for the pilot who destroyed the Death Star in this four-issue series by Darko Macan and Dave Gibbons (*Watchmen*). The story is available in its own trade paperback collection, and can also be found in the high-value, 336-page *Star Wars Omnibus: Early Victories*.

Star Wars Tales (1999-2005)

An ambitious experiment, *Star Wars Tales* took its "Infinities" label to heart by publishing a broad range of short stories from the likes of Garth Ennis, Peter David, Tony Millionaire, and Sergio Aragones. The series lasted an epic 24 issues and has been collected in a series of six trade paperbacks.

Star Wars: Union (1999-2000)

The wedding of Luke Skywalker and Mara Jade almost goes off without a hitch in this four-issue series, which was subsequently collected as a trade paperback and a limited *Star Wars 30th Anniversary Collection* hardcover.

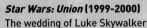

Star Wars: Chewbacca (2000-2001)

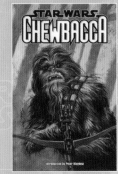

To commemorate Chewbacca's death, this four-issue series featured untold tales from Chewie's early years illustrated by Jan Duursema, Dave Gibbons, Kilian Plunkett, and more. It has been collected in trade paperback format.

Because the prequels revolved around the exploits of Jedi such as Obi-Wan Kenobi, Mace Windu, and Yoda, a risk always existed that prequel fans might eventually experience lightsaber fatigue. "In the prequel films, almost all the best protagonists are Jedi, and the few non-Jedi that we wanted to use—Padmé and Captain Panaka—were at the time off-limits for use in the Expanded Universe," says Stradley. "In hindsight I wish we had introduced more 'regular' characters, even though the prequels do seem to be about the Jedi and their downfall."

But Dark Horse continued to offer readers plenty of storytelling options. From writer Mike Kennedy came the five-issue *Underworld: The Yavin Vassilika*, a bounty hunter caper that sprang from Kennedy's love of Lando Calrissian. Also in the mix was the new ongoing series *Star Wars: Empire*, set during the timeframe of the classic trilogy. "Although I think the classic characters, especially the big three, have the potential to suffer somewhat from

short remembrances from early in Chewie's career as Han, Leia, Wedge, and others created a memorial to their fallen friend.

But the prequel timeframe remained vibrant. The four-issue series *Darth Maul* put a spotlight on Episode I's most popular villain, while *Jedi Council: Acts of War* put Mace Windu, Plo Koon, and other Jedi Masters through the wringer in a fight against alien aggressors.

The 2002 release of *Attack of the Clones* unlocked the era's true potential. With the Clone Wars, Dark Horse had an epic opportunity to deliver the gritty wartime stories that many fans had been craving, and writer Haden Blackman helped steer the course.

The Clone Wars were serialized in *Star Wars: Republic* (the new name for *Star Wars* as of issue #46) which established Asajj Ventress as a villain to be reckoned with. "This time period had an additional payoff when it became clear that Episode III was going to begin with the conclusion of the Clone Wars," says Stradley. "This left us a great deal of freedom to establish our own paths through that era."

overexposure, we didn't want to ignore that era," says Stradley. "My directive for writers working on *Empire* was that they try to show Luke, Leia, and Han through the eyes of other characters. Don't just show us Luke being heroic, but show us how he's heroic, and how his decisions and actions affect and inspire the point-of-view characters."

The 2005 release of *Revenge of the Sith* ended the live-action prequel era. Although Dark Horse published related tie-ins (including the four-issue *General Grievous*), it largely used the opportunity to take its stories in previously-unexplored directions including the Empire's formative years in *Star Wars: Dark Times*. As Stradley succinctly adds, "I feel very strongly that Dark Horse's job is not to reinvent *Star Wars*, but to simply tell the best stories we can within the existing framework of the galaxy." ☮

THE DARK HORSE YEARS

Star Wars: Darth Maul (2000)
The action is fast and furious as Darth Maul single-handedly wipes out a Black Sun criminal syndicate group in this brutal adventure. It can be acquired as a solo trade paperback, as a limited edition *Star Wars 30th Anniversary Collection* hardcover, or within the 454-page *Star Wars Omnibus: Rise of the Sith*.

Jedi Council: Acts of War (2000)
A four-issue series pitting some of the Jedi Order's greatest fighters against an army of Yinchorri warriors, *Acts of War* is available either as a standalone trade paperback or as one of the tales in *Star Wars Omnibus: Rise of the Sith*.

Underworld: The Yavin Vassilika (2000-2001)
This five-issue bounty hunter romp stars everybody from Boba Fett to Greedo. It is available in a standalone paperback collection.

Star Wars: Jedi vs. Sith (2001)
Set 1,000 years before the events of the movies, this six-issue series was the first to flesh out the character of Darth Bane. It is available as a trade paperback and a special limited-edition *Star Wars 30th Anniversary Collection* hardcover.

Star Wars Infinities (2001-2004)

These "what if" stories retold the movies of the classic trilogy, but with twists that caused their narratives to unspool as alternative history. *Star Wars Infinities: A New Hope*, *Star Wars Infinities: The Empire Strikes Back*, and *Star Wars Infinities: Return of the Jedi* are each available in trade paperback format.

Star Wars: Empire (2002-2006)
This series ran for a total of 40 issues and has been collected in seven trade paperbacks—the first of which, "Betrayal," centers on a plot by Imperial Moffs to kill Emperor Palpatine.

Star Wars: General Grievous (2005)
Originally printed as a four-issue limited series, this tale of Grievous' plot to transform Jedi younglings into his personal cyborgs is available as a standalone trade paperback.

DARK HORSE: INTO THE FUTURE

AS TATOOINE'S TWIN SUNS FADED INTO THE HORIZON AND THE CREDITS CAME UP ON *REVENGE OF THE SITH*, THE *STAR WARS* MOVIE SAGA CAME TO AN END. WHAT, THEN, DID THAT MEAN FOR SPIN-OFF STORIES? WITHOUT THE INTENSITY OF A THEATRICAL TIE-IN, WOULD THEY ALSO FADE TO BLACK? DAN WALLACE FINDS OUT.

Defying conventional wisdom, Dark Horse Comics' *Star Wars* comics hit higher sales marks after the end of the prequel movies than they had during their run—setting the stage for some eye-opening expansions of the *Star Wars* Legends.

"In hindsight it shouldn't have been a surprise," says Dark Horse editor Randy Stradley about the sales surge. "We experienced a drop in sales when Episode I was released, which I believe was due to the fact that fans could get their fill of *Star Wars* from many, many sources. After the films, comics were one of the items that stuck around. Fans came back to us."

Dark Horse made sure that those fans had plenty to pick from. The company (which has held the *Star Wars* license since the early 1990s) has a solid handle on what readers wanted from *Star Wars* comics, but that didn't stifle innovation. On the contrary, Dark Horse continued to launch new series and explore new eras as it took the storytelling possibilities of *Star Wars* into infinity.

The most direct connection to the post-prequel era came with the comics *Purge* and *Dark Times*, which answered the straightforward question: "So what happened next?" Unfortunately for the good guys,

the answer wasn't pretty. Both titles depicted a Jedi Order on the brink of extinction, hunted to the ends of civilization by Darth Vader and the nefarious forces of the new Empire. "The stories are grim, which is a reflection of the state of the galaxy during this time," notes Stradley. "Episode III set the tone, and our stories are following some of that grimness to its logical conclusions."

Would different time periods offer up sunnier outcomes? Dark Horse tested the theory with *Knights of the Old Republic*, an ongoing title set between the company's groundbreaking *Tales of the Jedi* series and the popular Knights of the Old Republic games from LucasArts. Given Dark Horse's previous pioneering into the ancient past, Stradley wasn't worried about launching a series with no ties to the movies. "The *Tales of the Jedi* comics partly inspired the Knights of the Old Republic games," he points out. "We were pretty confident that we'd find an audience."

Knights introduced Padawan Zayne Carrick and the fast-talking con artist Gryph, while fleshing out the Mandalorians in all their battle-armored glory. Editor Dave Marshall remembers that the lack of familiar "movie props" meant that *Knights* needed to capture the saga's spirit. "We set out to tell a quintessential *Star Wars* story with characters no one had ever met before," he says.

"We were confident if we gave readers their fix of lightsabers, chase scenes, scoundrels, and starships, they couldn't help but follow their curiosity into this whole new corner of the galaxy."

But *Knights* wasn't the only time-shifted series on the schedule. Unlike the novels, which featured aging versions of Luke, Han, and Leia, *Star Wars: Legacy* took place a full century later.

"We moved past the end of the lives of the core characters," acknowledges Stradley. "But their deaths are in no way what *Legacy* is about, any more than *A New Hope* is about the people who died during the Clone Wars. Everybody dies eventually, but we're telling stories about the living." Central to *Legacy* is Cade Skywalker, Luke's troubled descendent. Cade's adventures take him through a revived Sith Empire and a galaxy transformed in ways both large and small, from lightsaber-wielding Imperial Knights to futuristic TIE fighters. "We were pleased that Lucasfilm allowed us to move ahead in the timeline," says Stradley. "For one thing, we decided to move in front of the novels' continuity wave."

Yet between these timeline goalposts, the two core eras of *Star Wars*—classic

and prequel—remained. Dark Horse had no intention of abandoning either.

For the former, the company cancelled its *Star Wars: Empire* title and immediately resurrected it as *Star Wars: Rebellion*, allowing for an increased focus on Luke, Leia, and other soldiers of the Alliance. To mark the transition, the initial storyline told the tale of Imperial officer Janek Sunber (one of the stars of *Empire*) and his conflicted past as Luke Skywalker's boyhood friend. The news that Sunber was the "Tank" character mentioned in dialogue from *A New Hope* provided an irresistible continuity hook.

"Believe it or not, from the beginning writer Welles Hartley had it in mind that

THE DARK HORSE YEARS

Since the conclusion of the prequel trilogy, Dark Horse's output has included some of its most ambitious projects. From the ancient past to the far future, these Dark Horse comics will prep you for the newest developments in the galaxy far, far away:

Star Wars Purge (2005)

Following up on events in *Revenge of the Sith*, *Purge* depicted the bleak world left in the wake of Order 66 as Darth Vader hunts down Jedi survivors. A one-shot, it is available in the trade paperback *Clone Wars Volume 9: Endgame* and in Volume six of Dark Horse's 30th anniversary hardcover collection.

Knights of the Old Republic (2006-2010)

Set nearly 4,000 years before the events of the movies, *Knights* put a spotlight on the Mandalorian Wars before ending its run after 50 issues. It has been collected in a series of nine trade paperbacks: *Commencement, Flashpoint, Reunion, Days of Fear/Nights of Anger, Daze of Hate/Knights of Suffering, Vindication, Dueling Ambitions, Destroyer,* and *Demon.* You'll also need *Vector* Volume 1 to get the complete run.

Star Wars: Rebellion (2006-2008)

With the prequel trilogy a thing of the past, Dark Horse turned its attention to the classic trilogy with this series (a renaming and continuation of *Star Wars: Empire*). To get the full run, pick up the trade paperbacks *My Brother, My Enemy, The Ahakista Gambit, Small Victories,* and *Vector* Volume 2.

Star Wars: Legacy (2006 onward)

This innovative series is set more than 130 years after the movies and stars Cade Skywalker, a descendent of Luke's. Multiple collections exist, including *Broken* (which is also available as a standalone hardcover and as volume 12 in Dark Horse's 30th anniversary hardcover collection), *Shards, Claws of the Dragon, Alliance, The Hidden Temple, Vector* volume 2, *Storms, Tatooine,* and *Monster.*

Star Wars: Dark Times (2006 onward)

Picking up where Order 66 left off, *Dark Times* tells the bleak story of Jedi survivors with no remaining safe havens. The story has been collected in the trade paperbacks *The Path to Nowhere, Parallels,* and *Blue Harvest,* with *Vector* Volume 1 needed for a complete storyline.

---

eventually Sunber would be revealed as Tank," says Stradley. "Our idea from the start was to establish Sunber as a sympathetic character— a farm boy from Tatooine who had much the same upbringing as Luke but who had made drastically different choices about what direction his life would take. The whole time we were worried that someone would stumble onto the truth, but fortunately we were able to surprise our audience."

For the prequel era, Lucasfilm helped determine a direction with its focus on *The Clone Wars* animated series starring Anakin, Obi-Wan, and gutsy Padawan Ahsoka Tano. Dark Horse released two separate titles—a standard series and a line of digest-sized novellas—to coincide with the small-screen saga. The digests found an audience in bookstores, but the hit TV show hasn't had a magic touch on the comics medium. "I think that because *The Clone Wars* is perceived as being tailored for a younger crowd, our comics have not found as large an audience with core comics readers as I would have liked," Stradley says. "Eventually it became apparent that we couldn't sell enough copies to afford to continue. To a certain extent, we have to go where our audience is and give them a format they want."

Multiple series set across 4,000+ years of fictional history are great for reader variety, but could they ever be

tied together by a single narrative thread? Dark Horse accomplished that too, in the year-long crossover *Vector*. "*Vector* had its origins in a desire to bump sales, but we were determined that it would not happen unless we were able to craft a good story," explains Stradley. "It literally took us almost a year to come up with a story we felt good about." A Sith spirit and a stasis-frozen Jedi Knight provided the connective tissue for *Vector*, which ran through *Knights of the Old Republic*, *Dark Times*, *Rebellion*, and *Legacy*.

"We had a writers' summit where John Ostrander [*Legacy*] and John Jackson Miller [*Knights of the Old Republic*] came to the Dark Horse offices and hashed out the story from sunrise to sunset for several days," says Dave Marshall. "I think *Vector* came out as well as it did because of all the effort that went into making it something that mattered and not a throwaway stunt." Dark Horse got the sales bump it was looking for and fans got to see the comics in a new light. But given the scope of the project, Stradley isn't eager to tackle something like it again. "I really feel that *Vector* was the kind of crossover you can only do once."

As *Star Wars* rolls on, Dark Horse continues to diversify its line with *Invasion* (set two

decades after the films) and *Jedi* (set a thousand years before them). "We strive to never repeat ourselves," says Marshall. "We want to contribute something to the *Star Wars* mythos beyond a simple addition to the continuity of the Expanded Universe. I expect those will continue to be our goals far into the future."

Looking forward, Stradley promises that the only thing that won't change about Dark Horse's *Star Wars* comics is the sense of discovery that comes with near-constant change. "We're working on a number of new series, storylines, and shakeups of our line, not only for 2010 but the year after," he says. "2011 marks Dark Horse's 25th anniversary, and we're planning for *Star Wars* to be a big part of our celebration."

THE DARK HORSE YEARS

Star Wars: Vector (2008)
Dark Horse's first *Star Wars* crossover involved four titles, a year of publishing time, and more than 4,000 years of in-universe adventuring. The saga runs through four issues of *Knights of the Old Republic*, two issues of *Dark Times*, two issues of *Rebellion*, and four issues of *Legacy*. Two trade paperbacks, labeled Volume 1 and Volume 2, collect the story.

The Force Unleashed (2008)
2008's biggest gaming release came with a comic tie-in written by the game's own scripter, Haden Blackman. *The Force Unleashed* is a 104-page standalone graphic novel.

Star Wars: The Clone Wars (2008–2010)
Conceived as a tie-in with the animated series, *Star Wars: The Clone Wars* was scripted by series writer Henry Gilroy. The first six issues detail Anakin and Ahsoka's run-in with Zygerrian pirates and are collected in *Slaves of the Republic*. Six more issues have been published in the story arcs "In the Service of the Republic" and "Hero of the Confederacy."

Star Wars: The Clone Wars (digest) (2008 onward)
These digest-sized adventures are designed as standalone volumes. Four were published: *Shipyards of Doom*, *Crash Course*, *Wind Riders of Taloraan*, and *The Colossus of Destiny*.

Star Wars Adventures (2009 onward)
Like the *Clone Wars* digests but set during the classic trilogy, these tales include *Han Solo and the Hollow Moon of Khorya*, *Princess Leia and the Royal Ransom*, and *Luke Skywalker and the Treasure of the Dragonsnakes*.

Star Wars: The Old Republic (2009 onward)
Originally published online, this compendium of comics stories (under the title *Threat of Peace*) provides the backdrop for the forthcoming The Old Republic MMORPG game.

Star Wars: Invasion (2009 onward)
The galaxy is attacked by alien barbarians in this new ongoing series. One trade paperback, *Refugees*, collects the initial run.

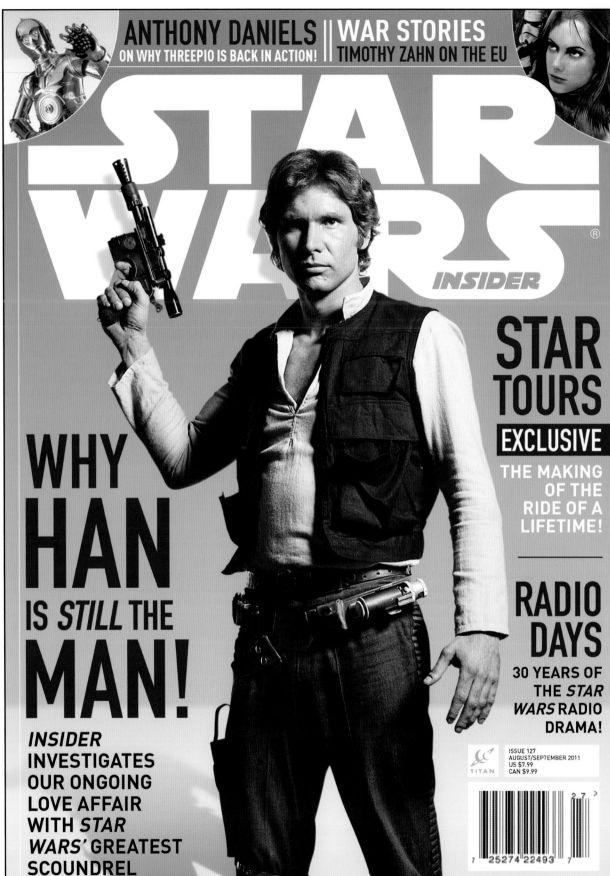

ANTHONY DANIELS
ON WHY THREEPIO IS BACK IN ACTION!

WAR STORIES
TIMOTHY ZAHN ON THE EU

STAR WARS
INSIDER

STAR TOURS

EXCLUSIVE

THE MAKING OF THE RIDE OF A LIFETIME!

WHY HAN IS *STILL* THE MAN!

INSIDER INVESTIGATES OUR ONGOING LOVE AFFAIR WITH *STAR WARS'* GREATEST SCOUNDREL

RADIO DAYS

30 YEARS OF THE *STAR WARS* RADIO DRAMA!

TITAN

ISSUE 127
AUGUST/SEPTEMBER 2011
US $7.99
CAN $9.99

7 25274 22493 7

SEARCHING FOR THE ROCKETMAN
STAR WARS TOY PROTOTYPES

ISSUE 127
AUGUST/SEPTEMBER 2011

THIS MONTH, FAR, FAR AWAY....

Star Wars: Dark Times: Out of the Wilderness 1 released

Star Wars Fate of the Jedi: Ascension released

Star Wars: Invasion: Revelations 2 released

Star Wars: The Old Republic: The Lost Suns 3 released

Star Wars: The Clone Wars: Incredible Vehicles released

Star Wars: Knight Errant: Deluge 1 released

Star Wars: Jedi:The Dark Side 4 released

Star Wars: The Force Unleashed II paperback released

Star Wars Adventures: Chewbacca and the Slavers of the Shadowlands released

What could be more collectible than *Star Wars* toys? How about prototype versions of toys that were never released? Gus Lopez, who created this intriguing feature, is a leading collector of *Star Wars* items. His self-published reference books on prototype figures are handy guides for anyone looking to start this highly specialized hobby, and his columns for *Star Wars Insider* detailing rare items from around the world underline the global reach of the franchise.

Of course, we had to include the infamous rocket-firing Boba Fett in this fascinating look at the toys that didn't quite make it onto toy shelves. It's always been one of my favorite bits of collecting lore!—**Jonathan Wilkins**

SEARCHING FOR THE ROC

The vintage Kenner Products *Star Wars* toy line remains at the core of *Star Wars* collecting interest today. Kenner pioneered small-scale action figures and licensed movie toys in 1977, and their impact had a lasting effect years later as nostalgia drew new collectors. Some especially avid fans enjoy researching toy concepts that Kenner pursued but that were never released for a variety of reasons, including production costs, waning interest, or better designs. Collectors refer to these as "prototypes," although the term is also used broadly to refer to any non-production item that played a role in the design and creation of toys that actually make it to stores. *Star Wars* concept toy prototypes were never sold by Kenner directly and are among the rarest and most in-demand collectibles from the vintage years.

KET MAN

A TOY THAT'S HARD TO SWALLOW!

The quintessential *Star Wars* prototype is the Rocket-Firing Boba Fett action figure, often referred to as "Rocket Fett." In late 1978, Kenner began promoting its first action figure mail-away offer for this mysterious bounty hunter from the upcoming *Star Wars* sequel, *The Empire Strikes Back*. In a heavily promoted offer, Boba Fett was featured on action figure card backs and store displays showing a rocket-firing mechanism on his backpack. Due to safety concerns that emerged from internal testing at Kenner, and prominent news stories about kids swallowing plastic missiles from Mattel's *Battlestar Galactica* toys, Kenner canceled plans for the firing backpack.

So the rocket-firing version was never shipped to customers and exists only in prototype form. There are two main variations of Rocket Fett, referred to as the L-slot and J-slot designs based on the shape of the slot on the backpack for the missile's trigger. The initial L-slot was considered flawed because just a light touch could easily fire the small plastic rocket. The J-slot allowed the slider to lock into position, but the bottom portion of the "J" could easily break off, creating an entirely different safety hazard. It is estimated that several dozen of each form of Rocket Fett exist today. The nostalgia around the figure is so widespread that Kenner successor Hasbro did a mail-away offer for a retro vintage rocket-firing Boba Fett last year as homage to the legendary promotion.

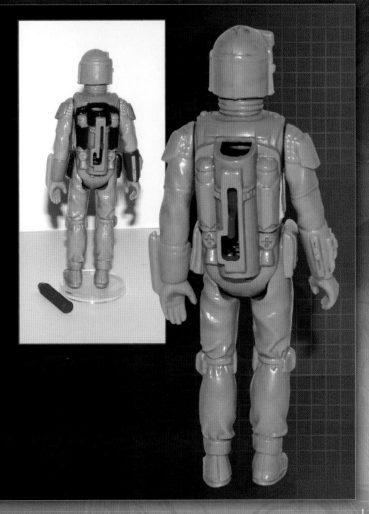

TALKING TO THREEPIO

Retailers would occasionally receive literature for upcoming *Star Wars* toys that never made it to market. One example is the C-3PO walkie talkies promoted in Kenner pamphlets for toy buyers in the late 1970s. Although initial prototypes were constructed, and details such as packing assortments, cost, and dimensions were finalized, the toy never went into distribution.

The whereabouts of the prototype seen in photos isn't known, although some blueprints, drawings, and photographs have made it into private collections.

BREAKING THE MOLD

Kenner's Micro Collection figures were sculpted at four times the scale of the finished product and called "4-ups". Some prototypes of these figures can be found in this scale as wax sculpts, urethane hard copies, or silicone molds. Examples of unproduced characters discovered in this scale include a Gamorrean Guard, Power Droid, and C-3PO from the Jabba playsets, and Luke's X-wing from Dagobah.

SMALL WARS

Another toy concept under early consideration by Kenner was a *Star Wars* pre-school toy line: non-posable figures and simple vehicles that would appeal to small kids. Initial hand-made prototypes were created for Luke Skywalker, Princess Leia, R2-D2, and C-3PO figures to sit inside a landspeeder and X-wing vehicle. Only one set of finished prototypes was made.

Although Kenner reconsidered the concept several times through the early 1980s, it eventually was abandoned. It wasn't until years later that Kenner came out with its first *Star Wars* pre-school toys, for the *Ewoks* cartoon series.

BLASTERS AND LIGHTSABERS

Kenner would frequently reuse an existing toy to design another, saving on tooling costs while introducing a popular new toy. One example was the Han Solo blaster squirt gun which was formed by modifying a Han Solo electronic blaster toy with a hollow cavity to form a reservoir for water. A pull of the trigger blasted water out of the barrel. However, this great summer toy was never produced. For *The Empire Strikes Back*, Kenner introduced The Force Lightsaber, which was a simple toy with a hollow channel that made a sound when the lightsaber was swung in motion. A modified "gyroscopic" version of the lightsaber was shown to retailers at Toy Fair and advertised in Kenner literature. The gyro lightsaber had a sound and motion effect, and multiple working prototypes of this toy were made before the concept was abandoned.

SMALL SETS

During the *Empire* release, Kenner introduced the Micro Collection line of small-scale interlocking playsets from *A New Hope* and *The Empire Strikes Back*, complete with inch-high, metal figures. Kenner had several playsets featuring Hoth, Bespin, and the Death Star in the initial release, with plans to expand with additional Hoth and Bespin sets to tie in with the upcoming release of a *Return of the Jedi* playset. The Hoth environment, and Bespin Torture Chamber playset were both shown in retailer literature, but Kenner decided to cancel the line. For Jabba's Palace from *Return of the Jedi*, Throne Room, Dungeon, and Rancor Pit playsets were in the works with new metal figures from the film. Only the Throne Room and Dungeon playsets are known to exist in prototype form today. Other Micro Collection playsets planned for *Return of the Jedi* included a Death Star Emperor's Throne Room and an Endor playset. From *Empire*, a Dagobah playset was also in the planning stages.

Luke and Leia model costumes not seen in the movies!

Leia, Han, and Luke prototypes for the cancelled *Empire Strikes Back* line.

TALL STORIES

It's hard to imagine that any *Star Wars* toy idea could be rejected, but as Kenner experimented with various concepts, gained experience with the toys from the first movie, and observed the phenomenal success of the small-scale action figure line that cannibalized sales of all other *Star Wars* toys, some outstanding toy concepts were inevitably left behind. Kenner had released large-sized action figures (approximately a foot tall) for the first movie and had plans to continue the line for *The Empire Strikes Back* with new characters from the film, such as Lando Calrissian, and updated outfits for Han,

Luke, and Leia. Although Kenner did produce large size action figures for bounty hunters IG-88 and Boba Fett, the other characters from *Empire* were never sold.

However, a wonderfully detailed sculpted head for Lando was made for the new figure and some hand-sewn outfits were created. Han received an updated outfit from his Hoth adventures, and Luke and Leia got outfits based on their visit to Bespin. These new outfits came extremely close to release with production box flats constructed and ordering literature sent to retailers. However, Kenner realized that

the small action figures were such an overwhelming success based on their lower price points and wider range that the higher cost large-scale action figures were phased out before these amazing new toys hit the market. Kenner had also been experimenting with new outfits for the Luke and Leia action figures that would be sold separately. Other than Luke's X-wing and Ceremonial outfits, the costumes were based on a fantasy fashion line not seen in the movies. Similar to the *Empire* large-sized figures, these outfits were made by hand in limited numbers and never offered in stores.

DISAPPEARING JEDI MASTER

Several other concepts for *The Empire Strikes Back* were rejected in the approval process. An extremely well-designed talking Yoda doll went through various stages of prototyping before the idea fell through. Using technology from the time, a pull-string would activate a voice box with recorded Yoda lines from *Empire*. The cloth body and plastic head and limbs were well-proportioned to create this plush Yoda. Also abandoned was a large Yoda hand puppet with a rotocast plastic head and plush

body. Due to cost considerations, the toy was rejected in favor of a simpler and smaller plastic Yoda puppet.

In the early 1980s, handheld LED electronic games produced by Kenner's competitors, Mattel and Coleco, were all the rage, and Kenner explored creating small handheld games for *Empire*. Paintings were made for the game backdrops using three different settings from the film, but Kenner eventually decided not to introduce the game.

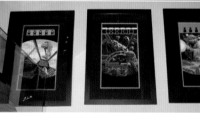

FUN AND GAMES

Although many toys were released for *Return of the Jedi*, a number of examples of unused toy concepts have surfaced.

While technically not an unproduced action figure, an early version of Luke in his Jedi outfit shows Luke in Jedi robes unlike anything seen on screen in the movie. The figure was later changed to come bundled with a cloth cloak. A similar early version of the Emperor shows the figure lacking the hood that was later molded onto the figure.

Kenner's affiliate, Parker Brothers, designed a game called Death Star Battle that recreated the adventures of Luke's attack on the Death Star using (or not using) his targeting computer. A working prototype of the electronic game was created along with hand-drawn box artwork. Although never released, it was fairly advanced for its time.

Late in the *Star Wars* line, Kenner experimented with "kit-bashed" action figures, formed by taking existing toys and adding other toy or model parts to create new concepts. Examples include a version of the R2-D2 figure with sound chip and a Leia as Boushh figure with backpack-mounted rocket.

DARK TIMES

In 1985, Kenner's "Power of the Force" line was the last hurrah for the vintage *Star Wars* movie toys. Although an initial wave of figures and vehicles was released with the "Power of the Force" logo, many new and reissued toys were planned that would never see the light of day. These include action figures that were to be reissued on a "Power of the Force" card but were only made as photographic samples for the 1985 Toy Fair catalog. Other examples include A-wing vehicle packaging (later released for the *Droids* television series) and a "Power of the Force" laser rifle. The figures themselves came bundled with aluminum coins; there were 62 in the set. Kenner had planned a special coin album and 63rd coin mail-away offer that was to appear on 93-back action figure cards (named because they feature 93 action figures on the back), but the album and coin only made it to prototype form before the line was canceled as interest in *Star Wars* faded.

TITAN

Issue 123
FEB/MAR 2011
US $6.99
CAN $7.99

0 9 >

0 74470 22493 8

BEN BURTT AND MATTHEW WOOD

ADVENTURES IN SOUND

ISSUE 123

FEBRUARY 2011

THIS MONTH, FAR, FAR AWAY....

Star Wars: The Clone Wars "Nightsisters," "Monster," "Witches of the Mist," and "Overlords" aired on Cartoon Network

Star Wars: Knight Errant: "Aflame 4" released

Star Wars: The Clone Wars: R2 to the Rescue released

Star Wars: Darth Vader and the Lost Command 1 released

*Star Wars: **Legacy: War 2*** released

Much has been written about the amazing sound design that Ben Burtt created for the *Star Wars* saga. Somehow, however, he always has a new revelation about his work; a new source for a sound that we haven't heard before. I recall a number of years ago he revealed to me that the Garindan (Long Snoot) informer during the Mos Eisley escape scenes in *A New Hope* was in fact a sped up recording of John Wayne.

Matthew Wood, who in many ways is Ben's protégé, has also proved to be a crucial part of the *Star Wars* sound over the years, whether with his innovative sound editing or as numerous voices in the prequel era and subsequent productions.—**Jonathan Wilkins**

Benjamin "Ben" Burtt, Jr. (born July 12, 1948) is the sound designer on various movies, including all of the Star Wars *and* Indiana Jones *films. Away from Lucasfilm, his work can be heard on* Invasion of the Body Snatchers *(1978),* E.T. the Extra-Terrestrial *(1982),* WALL-E *(2008), and* Star Trek *(2009).*

Matthew Russell Wood (born August 15, 1972) is currently the supervising sound editor at Skywalker Sound. As a voice actor, he is best known for his role as General Grievous in Revenge of the Sith *and* Star Wars: The Clone Wars. *He also plays battle droids, Wat Tambor, HELIOS-3D, Senate Guards, a commando droid, and Poggle the Lesser in the animated series. In 2016, Wood received an Oscar nomination for his work on* Star Wars: The Force Awakens.

ADVEN SOUND

THREE ACCOMPLISHED LUCASFILM SOUND DESIGNERS ASSEMBLED ON ONE STAGE TO SPEAK WITH FANS AT *STAR WARS* CELEBRATION V IN ORLANDO, FLORIDA. BEN BURTT, PIONEERING SOUND DESIGNER FOR THE *STAR WARS* AND *INDIANA JONES* FILMS, SAT DOWN WITH MATTHEW WOOD, SUPERVISING SOUND EDITOR FOR THE *STAR WARS* PREQUEL TRILOGY AND *THE CLONE WARS* ANIMATED SERIES. DAVID COLLINS, LEAD SOUND DESIGNER AND VOICE DIRECTOR AT LUCASARTS, HOSTED THE EVENT AND CONDUCTED THE INTERVIEW. WORDS: TONY A. ROWE

TURES IN DESIGN

After creating the iconic sounds of the original *Star Wars* trilogy and winning four Academy Awards, Ben Burtt had already ensured his name was in the annals of motion picture history. When the time came to create the prequel trilogy, even the master found himself facing unexpected challenges: "In the early '90s, I became a film editor and director for about five years and wasn't keeping up with sound technology," says Burtt. "When the prequels started, there was suddenly this world called 'digital.' The old ways of editing sound with razor blades, glue, and rolls of film were changing rapidly."

Burtt found a guide into the digital world of *The Phantom Menace* in his collaboration with Matthew Wood. "I am indebted to Matt because he was the young, self-taught, kid genius. I got ushered into the digital age with his great help. He would show me how to cut sound with a mouse and a keyboard instead of a splicer.

He became my teacher, though he may eventually rise up and kill me!"

Wood remembers that time from a different perspective. "I was just trembling in my boots the whole time that I was working with the legend, Ben Burtt." Wood says." When I first started at Lucasfilm, I'd sneak into a restricted, archived library of sounds that were still on reel-to-reel tapes. I'd pull some tracks and listen to them with headphones while acting like I was doing something official. The carbon-freezing chamber [sound effect] was my favorite."

Wood first assisted Burtt in upgrading the audio equipment for production on the prequels. "I thought the job would only last a few weeks but now it's been 15 years since we first worked together," Wood reminisces. "I was honored to work with him. To be able to teach him something was fantastic because I got to observe and learn sound design, his work techniques, and how to work with the crew. He's really been a guiding light for me."

This first task was simple compared with the Herculean job of upgrading the sound library. They needed a system to handle some 1,200 new sounds for *The Phantom Menace* along with all the material from the original trilogy. Most of the work fell upon Burtt's shoulders: "I like organizing; I like every sound created to have a name and a number because you end up with hundreds and thousands of sounds. I got into a discussion with Matt to figure out a way to catalog everything in one new, uniform system. Matt made me sit down to type a name and description for each of the thousands of sounds to start a database. Up until that point, it was only written down in notebooks or on the back of tapes with felt-tip markers. We needed something in a digital form for archival purposes."

"He'd had an amazing library to make all these great [effects]," Wood recalls. "None of it was labeled. None of it was categorized." Only Burtt understood the library's organization and spent countless hours creating the database. Wood teases Burtt, "You were kind of cranky during that time. Now it is all done and never has to be done again."

All aboard! Burtt (left) on the set of *Young Indiana Jones and The Phantom Train of Doom* with cameraman Chris Bromley (middle) and director of photography David Tattersall (right).

Ben Burtt takes a moment during the editing of *Star Wars: Attack of the Clones*.

The EditDroid team flanks George Lucas (center).

In conference with Scott McLean (Temura Morrison's stunt double).

Working on an action scene on the Kamino set with Steadicam operator Brad Shield.

Wood doesn't mind reminding Burtt that his own show benefits from those initial labors. "Now it can all be used—and stolen for *The Clone Wars*." Wood says.

Although Burtt hasn't worked on *The Clone Wars* animated series, he approves of the continuation of his work. "My career has taken me away to Pixar and off into other, new films. [When] I walk back to my old room, which is now *The Clone Wars* room, the sounds I hear coming through the door all sound like *Star Wars* to me. I feel that I can totally trust them. The language of sound that was established, starting with George's ideas, is being taken further. The universe keeps expanding and the library keeps going. I was always hesitant to turn the *Star Wars* job over to anyone; I was very protective and kept close control over the sounds. With Matt, he understood the value of it and has taken over that job. I feel comfortable." Burtt says.

After the prequel trilogy was complete, the pair reunited on another well-loved space fantasy film: Pixar's *WALL-E*. Andrew Stanton, the film's writer and director, told Burtt that he wanted to create 'R2-D2: the Movie.' Burtt explains, "What he was saying is that he had a main character that had expressive sounds and wasn't going to speak in words that we understand. Fortunately, R2-D2 and the droids in *Star Wars* had led the way. Audiences have been brought up understanding robots, something that was ground-breaking when it was done in the first films. It allowed *WALL-E* to have a basis as a successful concept. After I spent three years on *WALL-E*, I got together with Matt to co-supervise the sound editing on the film. It came back over to Skywalker Sound, as all Pixar films do, for sound-editing and mixing.

"Matt also connected our studios that were separated by 25 miles or so. He found a way to have a broadband connection so that sounds and images on a screen at Pixar could be mirrored in the sound design room at Skywalker. We could play and review sounds over a distance."

At that time, Pixar built a dedicated sound studio nicknamed 'Soundhenge.' Even after his three years at Pixar, Burtt did not find his name on the door: "They put a plaque on the office that said 'Matt Wood.'" says Burtt.

From Wood's point of view, this plaque brought balance to the Force. "I had Ben's name on the [Skywalker Sound office] door. For the longest time, we both had our names on each other's doors." says Wood.

Collins next asked Burtt how digital technology changed his approach for sound design. Burtt replied, "Some things changed; some things did not change. The aspect of going out into the world around us to capture sounds for *Star Wars* stayed the same. Generation loss used to be a gigantic problem in the pre-digital days; an original sound recorded on tape went through at least 10 generations of analog

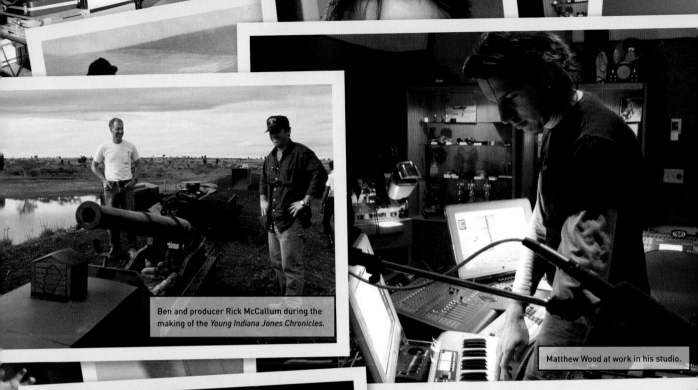

Ben and producer Rick McCallum during the making of the *Young Indiana Jones Chronicles*.

Matthew Wood at work in his studio.

John Knoll and Ben Burtt on the *Star Wars: Attack of the Clones* set.

duplication by the time it got to the theater. A great deal of effort always went into quality control and noise reduction or else sounds degraded terribly. With digital, that was no longer really an issue. That lifted a lot of stress from the sound editors and allowed them to focus on the creative. Another huge difference was that a library could be put into digital form to be browsed very quickly. We used to keep sound on old strips of film, sometimes broken up and hung on hooks. It took a long time to find a component for something.
A digital library can be browsed within a few seconds.

"The digital revolution for visual effects has [allowed creators to] synthesize models, textures, costumes, and characters in the studio. That kind of revolution didn't happen to sound. Sound is partly documentary filmmaking. The digital tools haven't allowed us to turn dials to create a voice. We still have to find those things in the real world. Digital made it much more convenient for us to do our work; more time can be spent on the creative rather than the technical," Burtt says.

Finally, Burtt offers advice to anyone interested in a career in sound design. "I find there are generally two groups of sound people." he says. "One group is made up of technical experts: they understand the latest software, know the latest microphones, and are passionately interested in the bleeding edge of technology. The other group is less interested in technology and more interested in: 'What kind of sound can I make by twisting this broken piece of leather around a wax paper plate?' They are thinking about how sounds can be used to give a dramatic dimension to a scene. Most successful sound [crews have members from] these two groups because they need each other. Occasionally, you find an individual who embodies both groups. As you are studying sound, don't neglect either of these areas.

"Build your own sound effects library. Get an audio recorder, go out, and listen. Here's my rule: If a sound catches your attention, like a broken motor in a grocery store refrigerator, record it. By recognizing it, you know that it stands out in some way and has a feature that is going to be usable later." ☻

Q & A WITH BEN BURTT AT CELEBRATION V

During Ben Burtt's panel at **Celebration V**, he answered questions from fans. Here are some of the best!

What is your favorite sound that you created for *Star Wars*?

My favorite *Star Wars* sound is the first sound I made: the lightsaber. I went out to the studio for one of my first [meetings] and saw Ralph McQuarrie's artwork on the wall showing these glowing sabers. I thought that was a fantastic visual. This was long before they filmed anything. I was a projectionist at the USC cinema department and I remembered the hum of the projection motors as I sat there in the booth. There were two of them and you could get a musical tone going between them. I thought, *Gosh, this is the lightsaber*, so that [sound] was discovered within 24 hours. Nobody challenged it; everybody loved it right from the beginning.

What is your favorite sound that you created for a non-*Star Wars* project?

I love gunshots, so I'm going to say Indiana Jones' pistol. In the *Indiana Jones* movies everything was exaggerated; pistols became cannons.

What are some of the oldest sound recordings that you have used in a film?

I've been going through all of my old tapes to digitize them, and have been discovering old things. I was working on the film *Munich* a few years ago. I discovered that I had recorded some propeller-driven passenger airplanes flying over my house back in the 1960s. That was just what we needed, period

sounds on recordings that were good enough to use in the movie. While filming *Return of the Jedi* in London, I made sure to record all of the telephones in the hotel and studio. Telephone rings change over the years as technology changes. I needed vintage phone rings and I had them. Sometimes the most mundane things are something you can snag for later.

What is the oldest unused recording in your library?

I have a folder on my computer called "To Be Filed." I like them, but I'm not sure what to do with them. One of them goes back to *Star Wars*; I made a loop out of a door thump that sounds like a heartbeat. I've never used it yet. ☮

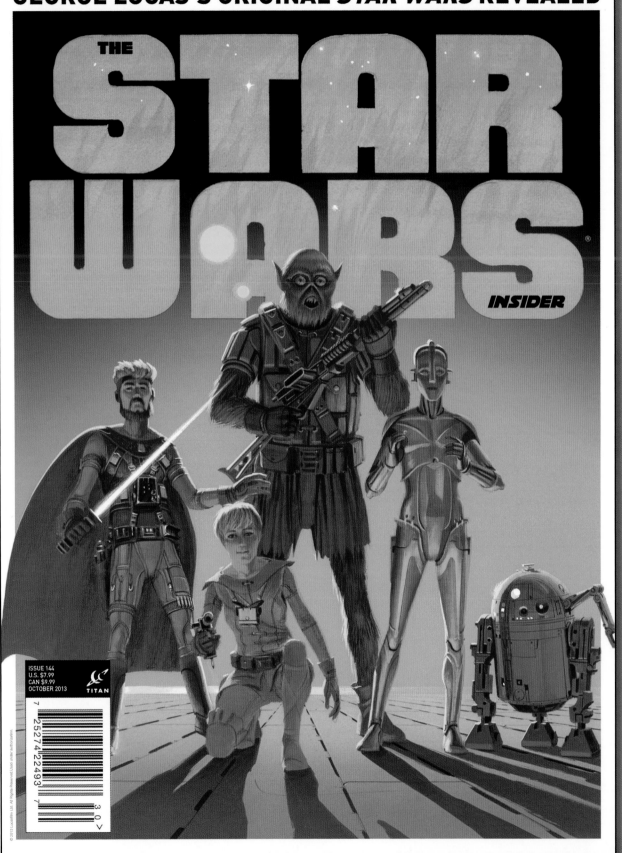

THE **STAR WARS** INSIDER

ISSUE 144
U.S. $7.99
CAN $9.99
OCTOBER 2013

TITAN

KNIGHTS OF THE OLD REPUBLIC
A MORE CIVILIZED AGE?

ISSUE 144
OCTOBER 2013

THIS MONTH, FAR, FAR AWAY....

Star Wars Art: Concept released

Star Wars: The Bounty Hunter Code: From the Files of Boba Fett released

Star Wars: Dark Times 31: A Spark Remains, Part 4 released

Ten years after it was first released, the astonishing Knights of the Old Republic videogame still felt as fresh and innovative as it did on the day it was released. It was, quite literally, a game-changer, having a crossover appeal that reached a far wider audience than just the *Star Wars* faithful. As ever with feature-writer Michael Kogge, we got a wonderfully in-depth piece that explores the impact of the game, which not only inspired a long-running and extremely popular comic-book series, but also garnered a whole new generation of fans with a 10th anniversary rerelease for iPad. I must confess to enjoying the game after a long day at the office. Sometimes you just can't quite get enough *Star Wars*...—**Jonathan Wilkins**

GAMING THE EXPANDED UNIVERSE

TEN YEARS OF

KNIGHTS
OF THE
OLD REPUBLIC

BY MICHAEL KOGGE

From left: Art director Derek Watts works on the game that would make *Star Wars* history; the groundbreaking graphics still hold up 10 years later!

Since opening in theaters in 1977, *Star Wars* has inspired a bounty of memorable computer games. Young fans of the 1970s fondly remember blasting X-wings in Kenner's Electronic Laser Battle. Atari gamers in the 1980s spent hours toppling AT-ATs in *The Empire Strikes Back* or reflecting blaster bolts in Jedi Arena. In the early 1990s, personal computers were transformed into X-wing and TIE fighter cockpits in intense starfighter sims. Numerous other games followed, taking *Star Wars* in different directions, from first-person shooter Dark Forces to the more strategic Galactic Battlegrounds. Yet one genre remained sorely absent: the narrative adventure.

Given that the movie trilogy was beloved and praised for its story, this exception seemed all the more curious. Played with pen-and-paper (which is what you use to play the game), West End Games showed that *Star Wars* could provide a rich narrative gaming experience in *Star Wars*: The Roleplaying Game. Why then couldn't the galaxy far, far away also sustain videogamers' interest with a strong, original story?

In 2003, Lucasfilm Games (later LucasArts) asked that question, and found no good answer. Of the 100-plus *Star Wars* games over the last 36 years, only one has landed on *Time* Magazine's 2012 list of the best videogames of all time.

That honor belongs to *Star Wars*: Knights of the Old Republic.

ABORTED ORIGINS

Knights of the Old Republic was not the first attempt to bring a more story-driven approach to *Star Wars* games. The designers at Lucasfilm Games (later LucasArts) made the company's reputation on highly original, point-and-click adventure games like Maniac Mansion and Loom, and they often discussed producing one in the *Star Wars* galaxy. But binding legal contracts kept those stars out of reach. "Lucasfilm had given the *Star Wars* license to other companies and couldn't make the game themselves. It wasn't until 1992-ish that they had the ability to produce them," says Ron Gilbert, creator of Lucasfilm Games' The Secret of Monkey Island.

Around that time, Lucasfilm Games had serious discussions with Origins, the videogame company behind roleplaying series Ultima. Designed by Origins' founder, Richard Garriott, Ultima was built around an innovative game engine that seemed well-suited to a *Star Wars* roleplaying game (RPG). Yet they decided against moving forward. The fact the Lucasfilm Games team had been unable to rely on the *Star Wars* brand for so long had fostered an independent streak among the designers. They wanted to continue to go on investing their talents in original concepts.

"With no more *Star Wars* movies planned," says Noah Falstein, co-designer of Indiana Jones and the Fate of Atlantis, "it didn't seem like the best way to go. The X-Wing series was a different matter; it felt like a perfect fit for the flight-sim engine we already had, and was much less resource-intensive to create than an RPG would have been. I expect we—or Richard Garriott for that matter—would have done a good job and made some money with a *Star Wars* RPG, but there were just many other promising things to work on instead."

> "WITH NO MORE MOVIES PLANNED, *STAR WARS* DIDN'T SEEM LIKE THE BEST WAY TO GO."

ENTER BIOWARE

The release of Episode I in 1999 renewed interest in a *Star Wars*-based adventure game. Tastes (and graphics) had changed since the early 1990s, and the LucasArts leadership recognized that the point-and-click games of the past would not sell in a more action-oriented, console-driven world. Moreover, their development slate was full with *Phantom Menace* tie-ins. So they made inquiries with a game studio that had achieved enormous success by blending an immersive narrative with the right amount of action to keep gamers glued to their machines.

Formed in 1995 by a quartet of Canadian med-school graduates, BioWare had spent three years in development on Baldur's Gate, an RPG that utilized Dungeons & Dragons rules. The game's major innovation was a morality system that would change the overall story depending on the choices the player made, allowing for freedoms more associated with the pen-and-paper RPGs on which it was based. The system also matched the themes of *Star Wars*, since becoming a Jedi necessitated making choices between the light and dark.

In late 1999, LucasArts' president Simon Jeffery contacted BioWare's co-CEOs Greg Zeschuk and Ray Muzyk about developing a *Star Wars* RPG. "As news spread through the company, it was a really exciting time. The idea of working on a *Star Wars* game seemed almost too good to be true," says Casey Hudson, then a technical artist at BioWare. "I remember talking with Greg about how I almost wished the *Star Wars* opportunity had come along a little later, when I would have been in a position to take on a leadership role—I had only been at BioWare for two years at that point. Several weeks later, Greg and Ray brought me into their office and asked if I wanted to lead the project."

Clockwise, from top: BioWare team members, James Ohlen (lead designer), David Falkner (core game design), Preston Watamaniuk (assistant lead designer) and Steve Gilmour (lead animator) in conference; fantastic characters, like Bastila Shan, helped garner the game multiple awards; Darth Revan and Darth Malak, characters who would transcend the game to become popular characters in their own right; the detailed environments give the game an immersive quality that broke new ground.

91

WHERE DO WE BEGIN?

THE TEAM'S FIRST PRIORITY WAS TO CHOOSE A *STAR WARS* ERA IN WHICH THE GAME WOULD BE SET, AS THAT WOULD DETERMINE MUCH OF THE DESIGN.

Accepting the reins as project director, Hudson assembled his team. James Ohlen, lead designer for the multiplayer RPG Neverwinter Nights, came aboard to head the design. Derek Watts was named art director, David Falkner and Mark Brockington lead programmers, and Steve Gilmour lead animator. Drew Karpyshyn, a writer for Baldur's Gate II and author of the Forgotten Realms novel *Temple Hill*, became senior writer. The team's first priority was to choose a *Star Wars* era in which their game would be set, as that would determine much of the design.

LucasArts gave them two choices: the period of the upcoming Episode II movie or nearly 4,000 years before, in the age of the Old Republic. Seeing what Tom Veitch, Chris Gossett, and Kevin J. Anderson accomplished in the *Tales of the Jedi* comics convinced BioWare to set their game in that earlier, "more civilized age."

The decision also opened up more possibilities to be creative. "By moving to another time frame, we were given a little more freedom," says Karpyshyn. "We had the ability to explore new plotlines and characters that didn't necessarily need to tie into existing storylines. It's hard to do something post-film and not, at least, talk about what happened in the films and to those characters."

Knights of the Old Republic, the subtitle for a 1997 reprint of the first *Tales of the Jedi* comic compilation, was found to be the perfect title for BioWare's game (which would in turn inspire a long-running comic series of its own).

BUILDING THE GALAXY, STAR BY STAR

The Aurora adventure-modding toolset that BioWare had developed for Neverwinter Nights made the hyperspace jump into the *Star Wars* galaxy much easier, because they already had a working game engine that they could tailor to *Star Wars*. BioWare also decided to keep using the Dungeons & Dragons rules, which Wizards of the Coast had adapted to *Star Wars* for its own licensed pen-and-paper version of the RPG. Not having to construct an entire new ruleset enabled BioWare's designers to focus on the content.

Out of all the films, the team tried to evoke *The Empire Strikes Back* most of all. Having the player character go through Jedi training became a must, along with offering the thrill of hopping around the galaxy in a *Millennium Falcon*-type tramp freighter with funny Wookiee and droid companions. In fact, one of the droids, the hunter-killer HK-47 (named after the initials of Karpyshyn's billiards team and the infamous Soviet assault rifle), surprised the designers with his broad popularity among fans, and went on to win the Game Developer's Choice Award for "Original Character of the Year" in 2004.

Ohlen additionally looked to his old West End Games roleplaying campaign for inspiration. "Zaalbar, Carth, Bastila, Canderous, and Mission were all characters from that campaign. The city world of Taris was also inspired by it, though it was originally to be named Sleheyron (after a world in my campaign) until I was convinced that it was a terrible name and changed it," he says. "Then I tried to sneak in a Hutt gladiator world called Sleheyron. That world was partially built, but had to be cut when we needed to trim content."

Not only did BioWare have to truncate story content, they had to reduce the size of their worlds. "We had built a lot of the levels, but they felt too large and empty," says Hudson. "The Kashyyyk level was so large, you could spend seemingly forever running through it. So we did an experiment where we scaled the environments down by 30 percent, which was a controversial thing to try, given all the work that had gone into building the levels at that scale. But, as we ran around the smaller test level, it actually felt like a more realistic space, so we spent several days scaling down the environments in the entire game."

Discerning players might stumble upon story strands in the game regarding a Tusken Raider and a "secret history" of Tatooine that has since been debunked. "We actually suggest that Tatooine is the ancestral home of the human race and that it was the Rakatan Empire that spread them to the stars. But that didn't make it into official *Star Wars* lore," says Ohlen.

NOT YOUR FATHER, NOT YOUR CLONE

The massive library of *Star Wars* sourcebooks and guides gave the designers solid ground on which to mold the planets and characters of this future past. But if they truly wanted to evoke *Empire*, they had to do more than build worlds—they needed an incredible twist in the story.

"One of the twists [*proposed*] was that the main character turned out to be some kind of clone," says Drew Karpyshyn. "Lucasfilm was already working on *Attack of the Clones* and that was one particular idea we put out there and they told us, 'Don't; that idea's out of bounds.'"

Suffice to say, BioWare discovered their twist by going back to the roots of their game system, looking within that very innovation that made Baldur's Gate such a highpoint in computer RPGs. The twist would echo the essential conflict of *Star Wars*, and for many gamers added up to one of the most unforgettable finales in computer game history.

AS OF 2013, KNIGHTS OF THE OLD REPUBLIC HAS SOLD OVER 2 MILLION COPIES.

Clockwise from top left: Greg Zeschuk and Ray Muzyka (execututive producers); thrilling combat is a key aspect of the game; as is exploration; unveiled at E3, 2002; Wookiee Zaalbar: but is he friend or foe?

NEXT-GEN KNIGHTS

Knights of the Old Republic had its initial release for the Xbox in July 2003, selling a quarter of a million copies in its first four days. The game would go on to garner numerous accolades across the industry and many "best of the year" awards. As of 2013, it has sold over two million copies on a variety of platforms.

Most tellingly, people have not stopped playing Knights. Nowadays, new gamers can first encounter the story by downloading a high-resolution iPad version adapted by Aspyr. Instead of using a joystick or keyboard, players can wield a lightsaber with the stroke of a finger. A testament to the game's lasting popularity is that within days of its release on Apple's App Store, nearly 10 years after the Xbox version, it climbed to the top of the iPad app charts.

The members of the Knights team have all gone onto distinguished careers. Hudson and Ohlen still work at BioWare, respectively shepherding the Mass Effect series and the massively multiplayer Knights offshoot, The Old Republic. Drew Karpyshyn is now a full-time novelist, having penned the *Darth Bane* books and an original fantasy, *Children of Fire*. But Knights remains close to everyone's hearts.

"When you make videogames for a living, there's always the concern that eventually people won't be playing certain systems anymore, and your work will be lost forever," says Hudson. "That's why it's always nice to see our games reappear on new systems, and the iPad version in particular is really special to see. I was playing it on the plane, on a device thinner than a book. Seeing that people are able to enjoy Knights of the Old Republic in new ways, 10 years after its release, has been a rewarding experience for myself and the team."

EXPANDED

Knights of the Old Republic is available from the Apple App store now!

UNIVERSE

STAR WARS

INSIDER®

HERA'S HERE!

Rebels Actress Vanessa Marshall on Fighting the Empire!

EXCLUSIVE!

JEFFREY BROWN!

Why Darth Vader is the Perfect Parent!

FANGIRLS UNITED!

How *Star Wars'* **Female Fanbase** Changed the World!

AFTER ALDERAAN

All-New Fiction Inside!

ISSUE #151
AUG/SEPT
2014
U.S. $7.99
Can $9.99

TITAN

FANGIRLS
FLYING HIGH

ISSUE 151
AUGUST/SEPTEMBER 2014

THIS MONTH, FAR, FAR AWAY....

Star Wars Rebels: Rebel Adventures Ultimate Sticker Book released

Star Wars Rebels: A New Hero released

Star Wars Rebels: Rise of the Rebels released

Star Wars Rebels: Ezra's Gamble released

Star Wars Rebels: Zeb to the Rescue released

Star Wars Rebels: Ezra and the Pilot released

Star Wars Rebels: Chopper Saves the Day released

Star Wars Rebels "The Machine in the Ghost" aired on Disney XD

Star Wars: Legacy Volume 3: Wanted: Ania Solo released

Star Wars 20 released

Contrary to what you might read in mainstream press, *Star Wars* has always been for everybody. Leia might be a princess in need of rescuing, but just as soon as she is, she rescues her rescuers right back—eat your heart out Julia Roberts! If the saga was just for boys, why is Leia so well represented as an action figure, and as a doll?

Once, when I was interviewed about *Star Wars* on a TV news show, the presenter actually said that she knew nothing about *Star Wars* as she was a girl! I was quick to point out, in fact, a large part of the *Star Wars* fanbase is female. It was this exchange that prompted me to commission this feature, from the ever-incisive Tricia Barr.—**Jonathan Wilkins**

Tricia Barr has been writing for Star Wars Insider *since 2012. She's written numerous stories on the hero's journey of characters in the pages of* Star Wars Insider, *from Darth Vader to Ahsoka Tano. She's the co-author of the first official* Star Wars *reference book in the new canon,* Ultimate Star Wars. *She is also a novelist. Her first novel,* Wynde, *was released in 2014.*

FANGIRLS

FLYING HIGH!

WOMEN HAVE BEEN SHARING THEIR PASSION FOR *STAR WARS* SINCE 1977. TRICIA BARR TAKES A JOURNEY THROUGH THE HISTORY OF FANDOM TO UNCOVER WHAT MAKES THE FRANCHISE SPECIAL TO... FANGIRLS!

What makes *Star Wars* so special to you? That question was posed to me last year in a context I never would have expected. Weeks before, I had experienced a brief moment of panic when I realized I would be out of the country for a family vacation to Peru and the Galapagos Islands on the day *Star Wars* fans celebrate the franchise. Despite the gnawing fear that I would miss having fun with my fannish friends or an epic news announcement, I reminded myself I would be swimming with turtles and penguins—and sharks, too, as it turned out—on May the Fourth.

As that day drew to a close, I sat curled up in the lounge, catching up on the fandom news in my Darth Vader pajama bottoms and *Millennium Falcon* T-shirt. Another woman from our tour had slipped onto the sofa, curious about what had me interested enough to surf the Internet after an amazing day.

The obvious subtext to her question was, "What makes *Star Wars* so special to you *as a woman*?"

On one hand, I'm used to the qualification: the media has declared *Star Wars* is for boys for as long as I can remember. My experiences as a fan since 1977 prove otherwise, and sometimes that sentiment elicits images of Darth Vader—upon learning that Padmé is dead—breaking free and shouting, "Nooooo!" That isn't the way of the Jedi, though. Having been inspired by *Star Wars* to tell stories, I would like to take you on a journey through time and fandom, where the ladies have been all along.

FANGIRL ORIGINS

Revenge of the Sith's shot of Darth Vader taking his first steps harkens back to the iconic monster in *Frankenstein*. In author Mary Shelley's introduction to the novel, she writes of the waking dream that inspired the tale: "Frightful must it be; for supremely frightful would be the effect of any human endeavour to mock the stupendous mechanism of the Creator of the world." Shelley wrote that when she was a teenage girl, yet her story ponders questions about humanity and tackles philosophical quandaries ranging from identity to free will. In the wise words of Master Yoda, "Truly wonderful, the mind of a child is"—as Shelley created a book considered the foundation for modern science-fiction. Shelley's lasting influence on pop culture shows just how much the notion that girls aren't interested in genre storytelling is blind to its origins. Franchises such as *Harry Potter* and *The Hunger Games* have come to the fore, written by women, and fueled by legions

"THEY LET [LEIA] HAVE A GUN—AND THEY LET HER SHOOT IT, AND HIT SOMEONE!"

of female fans who read the books, watched the movies, and were inspired to their own creativity. They weren't the first modern-age fangirls, though.

A PRINCESS WITH POWER

Maggie Nowakowska worked for a small publishing house in 1977. She had been immersed in *Star Trek* fandom, creating her own stories and interacting with other fans through fanzines and local gatherings. In mid-May of that year, Maggie attended the Library Association Book Fair. At the Ballantine booth stood an imposing black-clad figure to whom attendees gave a wide berth as they moved past down the aisle. Intrigued by the imposing presentation that revealed Darth Vader, she went with friends to

see *Star Wars* and left the theater thinking, *This is what I've been waiting for*!

When Maggie talks about *Star Wars*, it isn't one thing that struck her fancy. On Princess Leia, she noticed, "They let her have a gun—and they let her shoot it, and hit someone." Both Obi-Wan Kenobi and the *Millennium Falcon* were her favorite characters. Neither Maggie nor her friends believed Old Ben's story told to Luke Skywalker in his Tatooine hut, and they spent many hours pondering the puzzle of the Jedi's words. The *Millennium Falcon* was a place she could imagine spending her time, where she could fit her favorite books and zip off to different corners of the galaxy. *Star Wars* touched upon her personal passions of history and philosophy; she was enamored of the film's mix of myth and livability.

In the late 1970s and early 1980s, communicating wasn't as easy as dropping a tweet or email to a fellow fan on the other side of the world. Long-distance phone calls were expensive. Maggie exchanged letters with fellow fans, some up to 10 pages long. She read and wrote for fanzines, many of them run by women. Female fans, Maggie notes, were determined to get stories out with female Jedi. Just like male fans, they wanted to explore all the possibilities the movie left open: Was the Empire really bad? How did the politics of the Republic lead to the incidents shown in the movie? Were the Sith truly evil, or was Darth Vader simply a bad apple? Imagine, then, trying to have these discussions via letterzines, where the best turned around about every two months. For fans today—who can debate the motivations of characters or the inherent evil in an Empire in real time or at length on message boards—that kind of discussion lag would seem like a lifetime.

While the rise of the internet has its obvious advantages, Maggie's generation had experiences that today's fans can only dream of: fan trivia games run by *Return of the Jedi* director Richard Marquand, lunch at a film seminar with "Larry"—as in screenwriter Lawrence Kasdan—and others that make me too jealous to mention. In 2014, fans will likely only ever see a *Star Wars* screenwriter in a venue like Hall H at Comic-Con International: San Diego or catch glimpses of J.J. Abrams on television or a red carpet.

With the evolution of the internet into Web 2.0, hierarchically moderated message boards have given way to blogs and social media. Venues like Twitter and Tumblr have allowed female fans to

Clockwise, from left: The first lady of *Star Wars*, Carrie Fisher, strikes a familar pose; the first fangirl: Maggie Nowakowska at the start of *Star Wars* fandom; the new generation of fangirls; Jedi Master Aayla Secura in command; proud fangirl Adrianne Curry harnesses the dark side!

LADIES
WITH LIGHTSABERS

The saga has been shaped by many strong female influences over the years. By no means a definitive list, here are some key players.

Carrie Fisher (Leia, *Star Wars* original trilogy, Episode VII)

Marcia Lucas (editor, *Star Wars* original trilogy)

Carol Titelman (original Lucas Licensing editor)

Judy Lynn Del Rey (founder Del Rey publishing, publisher of *Star Wars* books)

Natalie Portman (Padmé, the prequel trilogy)

Ashley Eckstein (Ahsoka Tano, *Star Wars: The Clone Wars*, Her Universe)

Catherine Taber (Padmé, *Star Wars: The Clone Wars*)

Katie Lucas (writer, *Star Wars: The Clone Wars*)

Amy Beth Christenson (Concept artist, LucasArts, *Star Wars: The Clone Wars* and *Star Wars Rebels*)

Jan Duursema (comic book artist, *Star Wars: Legacy* and *Star Wars: Dawn of the Jedi*)

Kathleen Kennedy (president of Lucasfilm, producer, *Star Wars* Episode VII)

Athena Portillo (line producer, *Star Wars Rebels*)

Vanessa Marshall (Hera, *Star Wars Rebels*)

Tiya Sicar (Sabine Wren, *Star Wars Rebels*)

express their passion to VIPs, the fandom, and the general public in ways male fans have often taken for granted.

The interactive Internet is a double-edged sword, though. The collective fandom will never again experience anything as shocking and dramatic as the end of *The Empire Strikes Back*. Some of the greatest stories are journeys of self-discovery, and after the end-credits rolled for Episode V, fans had three years to ponder the infinite possibilities woven from Darth Vader's revelation to Luke Skywalker. Our response to a movie now is as much about the internet's reaction as it is about the actual experience. Fans tweet before they leave their theater seats while they are waiting for the end-credits teaser for the next movie.

A "RELATIONSHIP STORY"

Having observed the fandom from the perspective of an adult since the beginning, Maggie believes fans' perceptions of *Star Wars* are shaped by their first experience with it. My first experience with *Star Wars* was as a child. Reflecting on my own fannish tendencies, I'm inclined to agree with her. Tina Fey told Craig Ferguson in a 2011 interview, "What I took from *Star Wars* was kind of the Han Solo and Princess Leia relationship story. You know, they kind of like each other."

As a writer on *30 Rock*, Fey infused her stories with *Star Wars* references. Over the last few decades, female fans who engage in any franchise by expressing their affection for a particular relationship often have been met with derision. Being a 'shipper myself, the effect of seeing a successful woman like Fey admit that the Han-Leia relationship drew her to *Star Wars* serves as a reminder that romance is a natural way fans connect with stories. From *Cinderella* to *Frozen* and *Twilight* to *The Hunger Games*, two characters and their struggles to be together can create a powerful bond between fan and franchise. In that same interview, Fey shared her favorite *Star Wars* toy: the *Millennium Falcon*. I imagine, like Maggie, she might have created a few adventures playing with it. I've dreamt up a few of my own. Close in age to Fey, I know having toys didn't necessarily equate to meeting others who shared your passion. In interviews on my podcast Fangirls Going Rogue, both actress Clare Grant and clinical psychologist Andrea Letamendi admit to feeling isolated as children in their love of *Star Wars*, but, over the years, they have discovered many women with similar passions. Fast-forward 30 years and I had so many choices of *Star Wars*-themed apparel in my closet that packing for my trip to the Galapagos proved challenging. As it turned out, rocking my fangirl flair in a tour group was a great icebreaker. I didn't have to tell anyone I was a *Star Wars* fan; they knew it from my clothes—and everyone had a *Star Wars* story to share with me. By the second day, I'd made a new friend—a woman about Maggie's age—and, like Maggie, she was a longtime science-fiction fan, who never in her wildest dreams imagined there would be anything quite as awesome as the Princess Leia hoodie I was wearing.

FAN GROUPS

Considering this age of social media and *Star Wars* hoodies, it's remarkable how much in-person interactions still matter as much as they always have. At Celebration VI in Orlando, Dark Horse editor Randy Stradley told me about the Star Ladies, an organization that had been integral to *Star Wars* conventions and fandom.

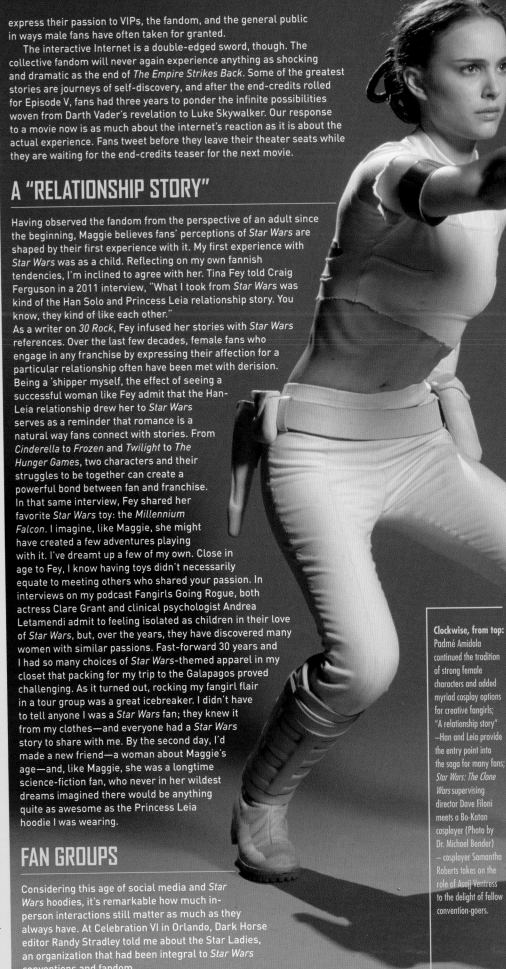

Clockwise, from top: Padmé Amidala continued the tradition of strong female characters and added myriad cosplay options for creative fangirls; "A relationship story" —Han and Leia provide the entry point into the saga for many fans; *Star Wars: The Clone Wars* supervising director Dave Filoni meets a Bo-Katan cosplayer (Photo by Dr. Michael Bender) — cosplayer Samantha Roberts takes on the role of Asajj Ventress to the delight of fellow convention-goers.

John "Dak" Morton detailed his trip to the 1998 Star Ladies' convention on the *Star Wars* Blog, emphasizing how smart and dynamic the female fanbase has always been, as the women shared their creative works and talked about the galaxy far, far away.

I met Maggie in 2013 when we both attended GeekGirlCon, an annual Seattle gathering to celebrate the female fan. At this convention, I met the most amazing women, including fangirl advocate Ashley Eckstein, voice of Ahsoka Tano in *Star Wars: The Clone Wars* and founder of Her Universe, a clothing company that has given girls and women the opportunity to flaunt their fandom. From the Star Ladies conventions to GeekGirlCon, female fans have been expressing their fandom in the same way men long have been acknowledged at larger conventions: cosplaying as Jedi, Sith, X-wing, and TIE pilots, stormtroopers, and bounty hunters; telling fan fictions like Kyle Newman's radio drama *Smuggler's Gambit* highlighted in *Star Wars Insider* #139; and sharing their insights on topical panels.

Each generation brings a fresh new perspective to fandom. Tracy Duncan, webmaster of ClubJade.net, shared with the Full of Sith podcast how she discovered the original trilogy movies on VHS over Christmas break in 1991, but found her passion in *Heir to the Empire* and the Expanded Universe. She was interacting with fellow fans on AOL forums in the earliest Internet days, and operates a respected fan-site that started as a fan-fiction repository and now covers news, speculation, and fandom. My *Fangirls Going Rogue* co-host Teresa Delgado proudly admits her best fandom moments were discovered in the prequel trilogy and has become an enthusiastic advocate for fankids. Journalist and longtime geek Amy Ratcliffe found her *Star Wars* passion during *The Clone Wars*. As part of the all-female Team Unicorn, Clare Grant has led the way in showcasing how women can express their fandom, either through fan films or exceptional cosplay. Andrea Letamendi has hosted popular panels about the psychology of cosplay and the parallel themes of *Star Wars* and *Star Trek* at San Diego Comic-Con, WonderCon, and GeekGirlCon.

Recently, I took another grand adventure with my family, although much closer to home. My four-year-old niece shares the same name as that original *Star Wars* fangirl, Maggie, and this trip was about creating her first memories of Disney World. Of course, a ride on Star Tours with a *Star Wars*–crazy aunt was inevitable. We laughed and giggled all the way off the ride, where we stumbled upon the Jedi Training Academy. My niece watched in awe as other children donned Jedi robes and wielded their lightsabers against the imposing might of Darth Vader—and she exclaimed, "I want to do that. I can beat him." Two days later, Maggie did. Her journey as a *Star Wars* fangirl is just beginning...

MORE TO SAY

Follow Tricia Barr on Twitter @fangirlcantina or her website FANgirlBlog.com.

HAVE YOU?

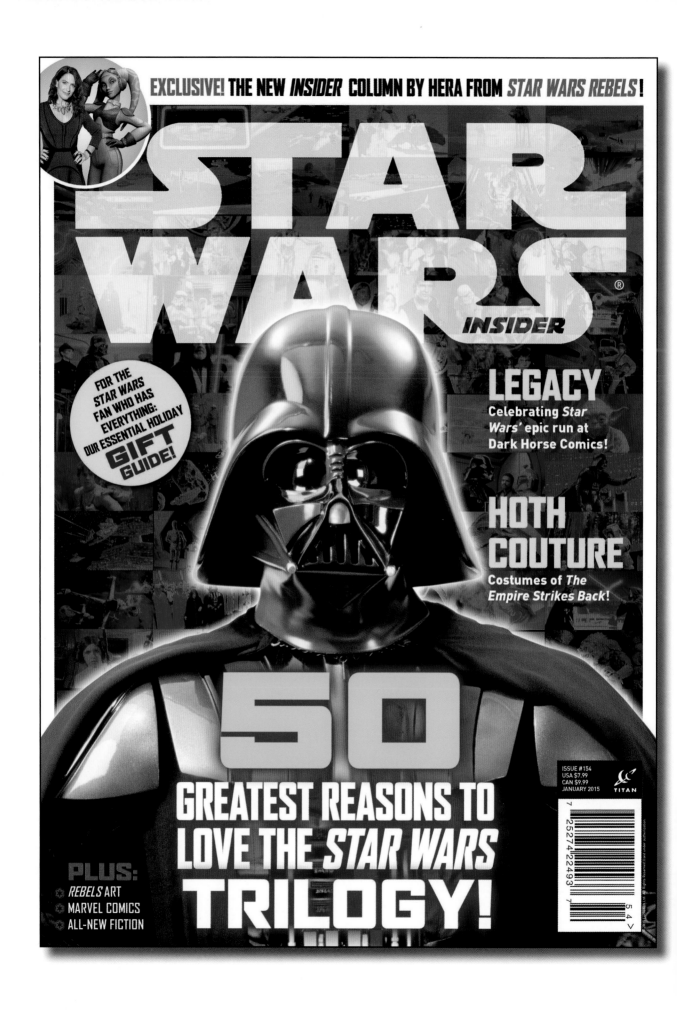

EXCLUSIVE! THE NEW *INSIDER* COLUMN BY HERA FROM *STAR WARS REBELS*!

STAR WARS
INSIDER ®

FOR THE STAR WARS FAN WHO HAS EVERYTHING: OUR ESSENTIAL HOLIDAY **GIFT GUIDE!**

LEGACY
Celebrating *Star Wars'* epic run at Dark Horse Comics!

HOTH COUTURE
Costumes of *The Empire Strikes Back!*

50
GREATEST REASONS TO LOVE THE *STAR WARS* TRILOGY!

PLUS:
- *REBELS* ART
- MARVEL COMICS
- ALL-NEW FICTION

ISSUE #154
USA $7.99
CAN $9.99
JANUARY 2015

TITAN

50 GREATEST REASONS TO LOVE
THE ORIGINAL TRILOGY

ISSUE 154
JANUARY 2015

THIS MONTH, FAR, FAR AWAY....

Star Wars Rebels "Path of the Jedi" and "Idiot's Array" aired on Disney XD

LEGO Star Wars: Vader Chronicles released

Star Wars Rebels: Sabine's Art Attack released

Marvel Comics takes over the production of *Star Wars* comics from Dark Horse

Star Wars 1: Skywalker Strikes released

Star Wars: Journey Through Space reissued

Star Wars: What is a Wookiee? reissued

Star Wars Rebels Magazine 1 released

Just 50? These are the most-cherished movies of all time, I thought to myself when the time came to create the follow-up to the well-received prequel version of this article, 50 Greatest Reasons to Love the *Star Wars* Prequels. Actually, this article was relatively simple to piece together, thanks to some wonderfully thought-provoking contributions from assorted personalities from the *Star Wars* community. As with the previous installment, there were no crossover suggestions and we didn't have to ask anybody twice: a minor miracle, believe me. We even had some wonderful entries via Twitter. The last one is probably my favorite.—**Jonathan Wilkins**

50 GREATEST REASONS TO LOVE THE ORIGINAL TRILOGY

ONE YEAR OUT FROM THE RELEASE OF EPISODE VII, *INSIDER* TAKES A LOOK BACK AT THE ORIGINAL TRILOGY. WE ASKED THE GREAT AND THE GOOD WHAT THEY LOVE BEST ABOUT THE ORIGINAL *STAR WARS* TRILOGY. COMPILED BY MARK NEWBOLD

1. FUEL FOR THE IMAGINATION!

I only have vague memories of seeing the first two *Star Wars* movies in the theater. I know I saw them because *Star Wars* made up every hour of my playtime, my school notepad doodling, and my imagination. My favorite thing about the original trilogy is the toys. My mom searched high and low for them. My brother and I dug trenches in the backyard to re-create the battle of Hoth. We even filled in some of those trenches with water to submerge our X-wing into the Dagobah swamp! Those toys gave me the tools to make my own *Star Wars*.—**Spencer Brinkerhoff III**, *Star Wars* artist

2. EPISODE V

For me, the greatest thing about the original trilogy is the groundbreaking special effects in *The Empire Strikes Back*.—**Danny Wagner**, special effects makeup, sculpting, and painting, the prequel trilogy.

3. HAPPY MEMORIES

I first saw *Star Wars* in 1977 at the Coronet Theater in San Francisco during the original release. I returned to the Coronet 20 years later to see the first screening of *Star Wars: Episode IV Special Edition*. On that very day, I was hired by LucasArts.—**Leland Y. Chee**, *Star Wars* Story Group member

5. YODA VS. R2-D2

In *The Empire Strikes Back*, there's a moment between Yoda and R2-D2 that always cracks me up with laughter. The Jedi Master and the droid have a tug of war over a flashlight. Yoda uses his cane as a weapon, bashing R2 while screaming, "Mine! Mine! Mine!" When Yoda gets what he wants, he gives the little droid one more whack with the stick and then laughs. It's so cheeky and funny; it gets me every time.—**Darren Hayes, singer/songwriter**

4. EWOKS

I'm a big fan of the Ewoks. A lot of people look at how cute they are and think, *teddy bear*, but they're missing the point. The Ewoks showed their true, inner savage nature in the forest battle, where they take on a battalion of stormtroopers with rocks and logs.—**Troy Denning, *Star Wars Crucible* author**

8. WHEN LIGHTSABERS CLASH!

One favorite thing? "But that's impossible!" I'm giving you two. My favorite line is, "You rebel scum." It sounds silly, but I use that whenever I can. My favorite moment is in *Return of the Jedi* when Vader learns about Luke's twin sister. Luke's anger fuels him and he springs from the shadows as the music soars and the vibrant red and green lightsaber blades clash. It ends with Luke telling the Emperor that he failed, "I am a Jedi, like my father before me." Hands down, it's the best moment in all six movies. I can't wait to see Luke again in Episode VII—**Erich Schoeneweiss, Editor at Del Rey books**

9. GOING BACK AGAIN AND AGAIN

There are so many—too many—things to love from the original trilogy that I'd find it nigh on impossible to choose just one. But there is one aspect of those life-changing films that has remained a constant over the years: their re-watchability. Every time I watch them, I take something unique away from the experience. Sure, there are other great films, other classic movies, other major motion picture events which hijack the zeitgeist and—for a brief time—become "as big as *Star Wars*." But when the dust settles and the smoke has cleared, there's always only one saga that's left standing, and that's *Star Wars*.

And the best thing? The next time I watch an episode from the original trilogy, I know it'll spark off another thought. It's the gift that keeps on giving.—**Mark Newbold, *Star Wars Insider* contributor**

6. WONDERING...

I loved all the speculation between the original releases of the films. After *Star Wars*, we knew Darth Vader had survived and wondered where he would make his evil return. What a revelation it was to discover, upon its release, that *The Empire Strikes Back* was not "*Star Wars II*" but actually Episode V. This further fueled speculation, as we now wondered about the mysterious chapters I–III. The years post-*Empire* were filled with more debate: Was Vader lying to Luke? Who is "The Other?" Will Han survive? Predictions, sometimes wild, were being made until *Return of the Jedi* opened and the saga was complete... For then, at least. Similar thrills were had during the prequel era and now, the ride continues as we look forward to Episode VII. So while "Always in motion the future is," I am happy, in this case, to see history repeat itself.—**Jimmy "Mac" McInerney, Rebel Force Radio host**

10. BOSSK

One of my favorite things about the *Star Wars* movies is the bounty hunter Bossk from *The Empire Strikes Back*. Other fans can keep Boba Fett; I always thought Bossk looked, well, like a boss. *Robot Chicken Star Wars* increased my appreciation for the odd, yellow-clad bounty hunter by making him a lover of etiquette. As the other bounty hunters are rushing out to find Han and the *Millennium Falcon*, Bossk—who has taken off his shoes—says, "Manners are their own reward, gentlemen!" Of course, when I was a kid I had the Bossk figure—it's still one of my all-time favorites.—**Ian Doescher, *William Shakespeare's Star Wars* author**

7. "ARTOO-DETOO! IT IS YOU! IT IS YOU!"

I love the bit when C-3PO and R2-D2 meet up again in the Jawas' droid slave ship. I really like the sad, silver guy with the robot-Russian voice.— **Peter Serafinowicz, the voice of Darth Maul, *The Phantom Menace***

11. BLASTERS!

I like how characters in the prequel trilogy handle blasters and lightsabers with ease. However, there's a certain innocence to the original trilogy in how weapons are handled. The handheld weapons seem to almost overwhelm the characters holding them at times. For example, the lightsabers were directed to feel heavy, and were wielded with two hands like broadswords. And when the characters fire their blasters, you can see them squint and react to the loud blanks that were fired on set. Compare Han Solo firing on Endor to Natalie Portman firing up at Count Dooku's ship on Geonosis: Their expressions couldn't be more different.

The same is true of how Luke handles his lightsaber in the original trilogy compared with Anakin's seamless lightsaber choreography in the prequels. I guess the original trilogy takes place during a time period that's simply less refined... or should I say less civilized?
—**David Collins, the voice of Han Solo,** *Star Wars*: **Commander**

12. THE ULTIMATE BOUNTY

The original trilogy came out well before digital downloads, Blu-ray, DVD, or even VHS were commonplace. So to a young boy who didn't have the luxury of being able to see the movies over and over again, my greatest *Star Wars* memories were the adventures I'd create (or re-create) on paper or through the toys.

The greatest achievement from that era? Acquiring the legendary 12" Boba Fett action figure on my seventh birthday! Not only was Boba Fett the coolest of them all, but he was the king of accessories! In addition to his nine points of articulation, this bounty hunter came with a rifle, belt, cape, detachable backpack with removable rocket, movable range finder, and braided Wookiee scalps! Best of all, Fett had a "sight" in the back of his head that you could look through to see his doomed targets!

Coming from a modest background, I never acquired any of the other large-scale figures as a kid. But let's face it, when you get a figure this cool, one is all you need!—**Matt Busch**, *Star Wars* **artist**

13. A CINEMATIC EXPERIENCE

At the time of the first release of *The Empire Strikes Back* I was working in Birmingham, England on a soap opera called *Crossroads*. A hefty work schedule prevented me from getting to London for the cast and crew screening, and the premiere. Imagine my delight when I received an invitation a few days after the London premiere to be part of the opening ceremony, featuring *Empire*, for the brand new Odeon Cinema in Birmingham. It had the latest projection and an amazing Dolby sound system. From the moment when the rolling opening credits were followed by the Imperial Star Destroyer looming menacingly over our heads, I was hooked. I was so enthralled that it was at least half a minute before I realized that my bit with Wedge, wrapping the cable round the AT-AT, had been and gone... And my voice had been dubbed!—**Ian Liston, Wes Janson,** *The Empire Strikes Back*

14. SALACIOUS MEMORIES

When we were filming the Jabba's palace scenes I was a young man, and like most young men at the time I had a very strong attraction to Carrie Fisher in her metal bikini! Unlike most young men, I got to be very close to her for hours at a time. In between takes my character, Salacious B. Crumb, used to pretend he was Gomez Addams and Carrie was Morticia from the TV series *The Addams Family*. He would start at her ankle, and slowly kiss his way up her calf saying,"Oh, Cara Mia! I am defenceless against your beauty." Then they would call, "Turn over," and we would have to go to work. She was always amused by Salacious's antics, but I couldn't help but feel if I had tried anything like that myself I would have been forcibly removed from the production. As we learned doing *The Muppets*: Puppets can get away with murder!—**Tim Rose, Salacious B. Crumb puppeteer,** *Return of the Jedi*

15. INSIDE THE *FALCON*

One favorite moment in *Star Wars*—there is no episode number on the original *Star Wars*, okay?—was Luke sparring with the training remote aboard the *Falcon*. Why's that? Look at the set—it's beautiful. Plus we get to examine a lightsaber in use. Han is hanging out being a skeptic. Obi-Wan is pouring on the fatherly mysticism. And to top it all off Chewie and R2 are playing a holographic chess match with little animated monsters! Just the absolute best mix of environment, characters, and effects.—**Howie Weed, Industrial Light & Magic artist**

16. RULER OF THE GALAXY!

I still wonder what happened to my *Star Wars* ruler! I must have been given it when I was eight or nine years old, and I used it for maybe three years before it vanished. It was blue, with the *Star Wars* logo on the front along with "May the Force be with you." There were images of running stormtroopers on the back firing their blasters. I used it so much that the red blaster-fire faded, and the edges became ragged and dented. I loved that thing. Maybe it still exists somewhere, buried in landfill or crushed up in the bottom of a box in the attic of a house I lived in years ago.—**Tim Lebbon, *Dawn of the Jedi*: Into the Void author**

17. YUMMY!

Salacious B. Crumb chewing on C-3P0's eye! —**Nick Gillard, stunt coordinator, the prequel trilogy**

18. COOL HAN!

My favorite thing from *Star Wars*: Han Solo's swagger!—**Phil LaMarr, Kit Fisto, *Star Wars: The Clone Wars***

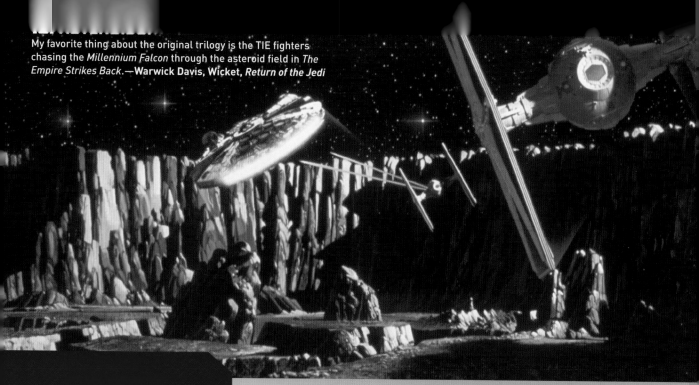

My favorite thing about the original trilogy is the TIE fighters chasing the *Millennium Falcon* through the asteroid field in *The Empire Strikes Back*.—**Warwick Davis, Wicket, *Return of the Jedi***

20. RAIDERS OF THE LOST JEDI

On the opening night for *Return of the Jedi*, my dad had arranged it so we could skip the massive line and pick whatever seat I wanted for the first screening. I loved the film, but the night was young. As soon as the movie was over, we had to rush off to a gig my dad had drawing caricatures for the 1983 NFL Champions: Los Angeles Raiders. I met legendary football players like Marcus Allen, Howie Long, and Jim Plunkett; but I didn't talk touchdowns. I was talking Ewoks, speeder bikes, and Jabba the Hutt! Most of the players just smiled and politely nodded, probably confused as to why this kid was rattling on about *Star Wars* and not the Super Bowl. Jim Plunkett, however, was really nice and seemed just as excited to see *Jedi* with his kids. After meeting the Raiders, we ended the evening by catching the late showing of *Return of the Jedi* for the perfect cherry on top of one of my favorite days ever!
—**Randy Martinez, *Star Wars* artist**

21. FIRST TIME

You can't replicate that feeling of seeing the first *Star Wars* for the first time back in 1977. And that film is different from the other two—it's more like *American Graffiti* in its giddiness. It's the most light-hearted but still profound, with Obi-Wan's transfiguration and Luke's initiation into the ways of the Force. You can't beat the now-legendary opening shot, the X-wings locking their S-foils in attack position, and the POV shot of the X-wing diving into the Death Star trench! On a more personal note, having George Lucas show me around his house, which from 1973-1977 was Lucasfilm HQ, pointing out what was in each room during that earlier period,

where the typist was, the make-shift sound studio in the basement, editorial in the carriage house—and talking to him for a few hours about that first *Star Wars*—that I'll never forget.—**J. W. Rinzler, *The Making of Star Wars* author**

22. THE SOUND OF *STAR WARS*

The *Star Wars* soundtrack was the very first *Star Wars* item I ever owned. Being one of the few pieces of merchandise available upon the film's release, it basically filled the emotional vacuum one felt after leaving the theater. I must have worn the record grooves pretty deep after playing it endlessly on our living room record player—a room, incidentally, which was off-limits to me as an eight-year-old except for the use of the stereo. One track in particular—"Princess Leia's Theme"—resonates the most for me, both nostalgically and for the sheer beauty of Williams' orchestration. Since the piece was used sparingly in the movie, it's become the most potent reminder of my childhood experience of the original *Star Wars*.—**Pete Vilmur, *The Star Wars Vault* co-author**

23. RED LEADER

As a fan of the original trilogy (dating back to 1977), I have a special fondness for the movie George Lucas calls Episode IV: *A New Hope*, but which I still stubbornly and unabashedly call *Star Wars*! I watch *Star Wars* at least twice a year, and every time I do, one character always tugs my heartstrings like no other. I'm speaking, of course, of poor, doomed Red Leader. He spends the bulk of the Battle of Yavin issuing orders to Luke, Wedge, Biggs, Porkins, and the rest of the Red and Gold Squadrons before taking the first shot at the Death Star's thermal exhaust port. Of course, he misses! If he doesn't, then Luke can't trust the Force, turn off his targeting computer and make that one-in-a-billion shot that sends him to the medal podium. But the hauntingly tragic way actor Drewe Henley plays Red Leader's sad, defeated, "Negative, negative, it didn't go in" never fails to put a Chewbacca-sized lump in my throat. Henley's performance of that moment sums up for me the humanity and genuineness that made *Star Wars* so special. Next time you watch that scene, I dare you to look at the hopeless resignation in Red Leader's eyes and not shed a tear. To me, it is the greatest piece of screen acting in the entire series.—**Michael Price, LEGO** *Star Wars Yoda Chronicles* **writer**

24. LEIA

I played Cordé in Episode II, a highly unexpected event as I pretended to be Princess Leia while still in elementary school! I remember adoring her braided hairdo to the point of envy, loved being disgusted by Jabba the Hutt, and really wanted to cuddle an Ewok! What I love the most about the original trilogy is the countless hours of play that it gave me with my brother and cousins.—**Veronica Segura, Cordé,** *Attack of the Clones*

26. PIGGING OUT!

Having hair dryers wedged into my Gamorrean gob to cool down between takes, because it would take too much time and effort to start dismantling the costume! I didn't like the KY Jelly for drool so much, though! —**Simon J. Williamson, Gamorrean guard,** *Return of the Jedi*

25. SAGA BUILDING

Salacious B. Crumb mesmerized by Jabba's tail... Oh, and Obi-Wan's Force spirit telling Luke, "I may have kind of stretched the truth... From a certain point of view" If only Force spirit Obi-Wan could have been sitting there with Salacious Crumb... Now that's gold!

The trilogy did something that no other movie sequels did for me: It forever changed my view of movie-making. They were each their own film while still being part of the same story, but they were each their own individual story. They didn't try to re-create moments from the previous instalment. They showed us

that sequels can have their own identity and that started something that *Lord of the Rings*, *Harry Potter* and every recent superhero movie can be very thankful for.—**James Arnold Taylor, Obi-Wan Kenobi,** *Star Wars: The Clone Wars*

27. IT'S HUGE!

The pure, ingenuous, eyes-open, un-ironic delight of Episode IV exploding onto the screen, and that opening visual of the Star Destroyer cruising into frame above us... and cruising... and cruising... and... Oh my God! How big exactly is this ship? —**James Kahn,** *Return of the Jedi* **novelization author**

28. READY TO ROLL

One of my many favorite moments on *A New Hope* was on the first day of filming in Tunisia. We were filming the line-up of droids to be sold to Uncle Owen and Luke. We had not had a lot of time to prep—the film was greenlit in December and here we were in March filming outside of Tozeur. John Stears, the special effects supervisor, had promised us all that he could have R2-D2 radio-controlled and functioning, but John Barry, the production designer, was skeptical and had Les Dilley and I make a lightweight mock-up in fibreglass we could pull along with fishing wire in case. This was used extensively after this first day. R2-D2 was supposed to move forward, in a straight line, and follow C-3PO. On action, John Stears (who built R2-D2) was controlling the radio and R2-D2 wobbled a little, went out of control and fell over. There was silence on the set. Suddenly John rushed in front of the camera and announced loudly,

"It's the bloody taxis!" meaning their radio frequencies were jamming his. This excuse might have worked in London, but we were 45 minutes into the desert outside the sleepy little town of Tozeur, which had one hotel and maybe a few old taxis, camels,

donkeys, and carts mainly as the transport. Out came our fishing wire-led mock-up, and little R2-D2 was pulled along for filming where we could use it without being seen—**Roger Christian**, *Star Wars* **set decorator/production designer**

29. LUKE

While Obi-Wan is my favorite character in the saga now, originally it was Luke because I identified with his yearning to break away, leave home, and get involved in the larger world—or galaxy—beyond. That had been my story, too. And nothing still brings that home to me more than John Williams' magnificent music cue, "Binary Sunset." A frustrated Luke walks to a small hill in the gathering dusk and looks up at the setting twin suns of Tatooine. Without a word spoken, you know exactly what he's feeling as the plaintive music builds.—**Stephen Sansweet, President and CEO, Rancho Obi-Wan**

30. EVASIVE ACTION!

For me, it's all about the Imperial Star Destroyers taking evasive action in *The Empire Strikes Back* as the *Millennium Falcon* dives away from them. First of all, it's an insanely cool special effect, with these huge behemoths trying desperately to roll out of harm's way in the background as the *Falcon* and the TIE fighters engage in a deadly ballet below them. But I also love the klaxons sounding aboard the bridges, and the panic in the officers' voices. You can imagine the dressings-down that must have followed, the paperwork filled out as part of bureaucratic incident reports, and the black marks on lots of service records. All this to chase a dented freighter away from some ice ball? Why, it's enough to drive a veteran of the Imperial Navy crazy!—**Jason Fry,** *Star Wars Rebels* **Servants of the Empire:** *Edge of the Galaxy* **author**

31. JABBA'S BUDDY!

My best memory of being on the Jabba's palace set was when Jabba had to look down at Luke in the rancor pit. Even with everything on maximum, Jabba couldn't quite make the forward lean. So David Tomblin (first AD) asked me if Jabba could be pushed from behind. I said yes, but the internal frame might jump off its springs and the sharp edge might burst the belly air bag.

In all the vast details he had to think about, David remembered visiting when Jabba was being constructed and knew what I was talking about. I also knew I could trust him to help us if anything did go wrong, rather than give us a bad time. He was a great guy and the best compliment any of us ever got was David pushing through us on set, with a backwards jab of his thumb to Jabba, and growling "You've done a good job on that thing."—**John Coppinger, Jabba sculptor,** *Return of the Jedi*

32. PURE WESTERN

I was 15 when *Star Wars* changed movies... and my life. An integral element of the original trilogy that I did not see at the time was pointed out by my then 80-something-year-old grandmother. By the time she came to visit in the summer of 1977, I had seen *Star Wars* about 10 times. When I told her about it, she said she wanted to see it as well. I was a bit surprised, as I just assumed no one her age would be interested. Boy, was I wrong! When we walked out of the theater, she said not only was it a terrific movie, but it really took her back to her favorite movies from the black-and-white era of Hollywood. When I told her (very politely) that she was

nuts—that *Star Wars* was a modern achievement, she told me I was wrong. She said that obviously, the people who made it were setting a tried-and-true story format in outer space—the old reliable

good guys vs. bad guys Western movie.

Of course, as time went by, and I learned more about George Lucas's intentions and inspiration for the original trilogy, I realized my grandmother was completely correct.

My grandmother has been gone for many years, but next year when the lights go down and the giant *Star Wars* title slams onto the screen to begin Episode VII, accompanied by the first notes of John Williams' explosive score, she will be sitting by my side, cheering for the good guys.—**Tom Kane, Yoda, *Star Wars: The Clone Wars***

33. JEDI MASTER

I hate Yoda's house! It's not suitable for an old man who is in ill health. But I love Yoda from Episode V!
—**Tsuneo Sanda, *Star Wars* artist**

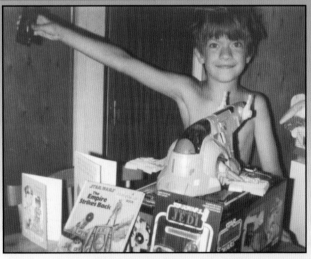

34. TOY STORIES

There's something incredibly magical about Kenner's—or Palitoy's, if you grew up in the UK—line of *Star Wars* action figures. I can still see the card-back figures lining the walls of my local toy store and can easily recall the potent feeling of excitement when a new batch of figures would arrive— especially when the figures in question were from a film that was yet to be released! Who was the mysterious General Madine? Was Squid Head—clad in familiar-looking brown robes—a Jedi? The crowning glory would be when, at Christmas and for birthdays, a new vehicle would be unpacked, to near hysterical levels of excitement.—**Jonathan Wilkins, *Star Wars Insider* editor**

35. TOPPS!

There is one thing that stands out to me: Topps' *Star Wars* trading cards. In a time when there were no VCRs to re-watch *Star Wars*, I treasured my walks to the corner market to pick up a pack of cards. I ceremoniously opened each pack and carefully inspected the photos, reliving the movie while chewing the brick of dry gum in each pack. It was my childhood sci-fi ritual and I savored every *Star Wars* morsel from those card packs.—**Albin Johnson, 501st Legion founder**

36. DARTH VADER

My favorite thing from the original trilogy was seeing Darth Vader appear for the first time on the Blockade Runner in Episode IV.

Star Wars was the very first movie I saw in the theater when I was barely four years old. The first time I watched this ominous villain enter the scene through the blaster smoke with the stormtroopers I was so scared I tried crawling under my seat in the movie theater. But I was as frightened by him as I was fascinated. I remember sneaking peeks between the seats trying to conquer my fear and catch a glimpse of this nightmarish character. I thought he was some kind of demon. Surely there couldn't be a man in there, could there? As I grew up with these films I knew I had to learn more about him, who was inside that armor, where he came from, why was he so angry and evil? To this day, Darth Vader remains my favorite character to work with as a storyteller and a creator in my Star Wars artwork.—Joe Corroney, Star Wars artist

37. HAIR DOS AND DON'TS

I'd never seen anything like Chewbacca before, but the sounds he made reminded me of how the adults sounded in Charlie Brown cartoons! Princess Leia's comment about getting the walking carpet out of her way tickled my funny bone so much it still makes me laugh to this day!

I was fascinated with Princess Leia's "hair buns." Years later I realized it'd be great to have Leia's "hairdo headphones" for my work in voice-over. I could be Forcefully fashionable in front of the microphone!—Tasia Valenza, Shaak Ti, Star Wars: The Clone Wars

38. SUPER STAR WARS!

I loved my Star Wars Super 8 color/sound 12 minutes of film. I watched it over and over and shared it with friends on my backyard big screen (made from a white sheet) on my home projector. My Don Post masks, which I displayed proudly in my room, which was covered wall to wall with Star Wars posters; and hearing Yoda say, "Judge me by my size, do you?" It made me realize that even though I was 4' 2" I could still be a force in the world.— Dan Madsen, Star Wars fan club founder and former Star Wars Insider publisher

39 FAMILY DRAMA

A favorite scene of mine from the original trilogy has to be when Luke has breakfast with his uncle and aunt. It's simple, a dining room conversation that grounds the entire space fantasy in a concrete reality. The motivations of both Luke and Owen are crystal clear—Luke's a young man with big dreams to travel the stars, but his uncle needs help on the farm.

As I've gotten older, I sympathize with Owen. What will he do without Luke's help? Droids can't do everything. Luke's also the couple's adopted child, and giving him up to the Academy will be hard, even for the curmudgeonly Owen. The scene becomes more poignant when compared to its mirror in The Phantom Menace, when Anakin expresses his own desires at the kitchen table to Qui-Gon.

For a movie loaded with special effects, the only effect in Owen and Beru's dining room is the food coloring used to create blue milk. I love this scene because it cuts right to the heart as pure character drama.—Michael Kogge, Star Wars Rebels: The Rebellion Begins author

40. HAN SOLO'S REVENGE

Blind Han Solo yelling, "Boba Fett? Boba Fett! Where?"—**Freddie Prinze, Jr., Kanan, *Star Wars Rebels***

41. CANTINA GIRL

I was an alien in the Cantina in *Star Wars*. Working on the film, I never knew what the script was about; it was just a job at the time. My makeup was three hours a day, and I did five days shooting and got two days overtime just for my makeup! I was called a few cheeky names whilst on set, and had my bum bitten by Kenny Baker! I did my knitting in the breaks and the one thing that was very nice was that I was allowed to take two Polaroid pictures of myself to show my dad who was very ill.—**Pam Rose, Leesub Sirln, *A New Hope***

42. IT'S WORKING!

My favorite thing from the original trilogy is having worked on it!—**Robert Watts, producer, the original trilogy**

43. SCHOOL OF YODA

My favorite thing about the original trilogy is Yoda's training of Luke on Dagobah, or what I like to call, "The School of Yoda." I have always felt that when I follow Master Yoda's advice in my own life things seem to work out. If you can't believe something and imagine it to be true in your own mind first, you will not be able to achieve it. And of course, "Do. Or do not. There is no try". We hear it quoted all the time, but it is powerful and if you live this way, you really can avoid regrets. Also, at 5'3", I'm quite partial to "Judge me by my size, do you? And well you should not." I feel exactly the same way! —**Catherine Taber, Padmé Amidala, *Star Wars: The Clone Wars***

44. STANDING ON CEREMONY

The music at the end of *A New Hope* gets me every time. I saw this movie in Walthamstow, London. I took my daughter and as the heroes came to collect their medals my daughter, who was five years of age at the time, shouted out at the top of her voice, "LOOK DAD, THERE YOU ARE!" I could not find a hole big enough!—**Nick Joseph, medal bearer (standing behind Carrie Fisher), *A New Hope***

45. EVIL DEFEATED!

The most elegant completion of a narrative arc: When Vader turns away from the dark side and becomes Anakin Skywalker again, destroying Palpatine and saving his son, Luke!—**Vanessa Marshall, Hera,** *Star Wars Rebels*

46. THROWAWAYS

I love George Lucas's throwaways. They are the great things that appear for a brief time and then disappear. Things like banthas and the Cantina patrons, for example. It made you pay attention.—**Alan Dean Foster,** *Splinter of the Mind's Eye* **author**

47. SQUEAK!

I love the original *Star Wars* to bits! The mouse droid in the hallway and the smug delight Chewbacca took in routing it pops into my mind whenever I think of my favorite part!—**Mary Jo Duffy, former Marvel Comics** *Star Wars* **editor**

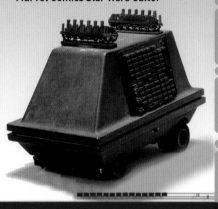

48. LIGHT SIDE WINS!

My favorite thing about the original trilogy is the message I take away from the movies. To me, it's a story of hope and of good overcoming evil. I cannot help but be inspired every time I watch these classic films!—**Ashley Eckstein, Ahsoka Tano,** *Star Wars: The Clone Wars*

49. ANYTHING CAN HAPPEN

It's hard to imagine now, but the original *Star Wars* generation had to wait over a decade to find out that Ponda Baba was an Aqualish. These days, the names and backstories of bit players are served up instantly, on action figure packaging, visual dictionaries or encyclopedic websites. But in the original trilogy days, the galaxy was uncharted, and it felt like anything could

happen. The nooks and crannies of the Mos Eisley Cantina, Cloud City, or Jabba's palace were filled with surprises, and cryptic names like Walrus Man, Hammerhead, or Tooth Face formed a springboard for imagination.

That sense of the unknown, of unanswered questions, was actually a key part of the experience. It formed the basis of schoolyard debate and discussion for years in-between movies. The prequel era brought with it a bittersweet trade-off. In exchange for accessible, authoritative

voices that settled *Star Wars* debates, we've given up some of the mystique and wonder that comes from the unknown. I'm excited to get that back as we head into new storytelling territory—**Pablo Hidalgo,** *Star Wars* **Story Group member**

50 ....

That pause between "A long time ago..." and the opening titles. It's always electric. —**LJ,** *Star Wars Insider* **reader, via Twitter**

2 OF 2 COLLECTIBLE COVERS!

COLLECT THEM BOTH! STAR WARS REBELS AND DARTH VADER AND FAMILY!

STAR WARS

INSIDER

HERA'S HERE!

Rebels Actress Vanessa Marshall on Fighting the Empire!

EXCLUSIVE!

JEFFREY BROWN!

Why Darth Vader is the Perfect Parent!

FANGIRLS UNITED!

How Star Wars' **Female Fanbase** Changed the World!

AFTER ALDERAAN-

All-New Fiction Inside!

ISSUE #151
AUG/SEPT
2014
U.S. $7.99
Can $9.99

TITAN

7 25274 22493 7

51

HERA SYNDULLA
VANESSA MARSHALL

ISSUE 151
AUGUST/SEPTEMBER 2014

THIS MONTH, FAR, FAR AWAY....

The Star Wars deluxe hardcover released

LEGO Star Wars: The Dark Side released

Star Wars Rebels "Art Attack," "Entanglement," and "Property of Ezra Bridger" aired on Disney XD

Star Wars: Darth Maul: Son of Dathomir, Part Four released

Star Wars: Commander released

Star Wars Rebels: Head to Head released

Star Wars: Legacy Volume 2 18 released

Star Wars: A New Dawn released

Draw Star Wars Rebels released

The actress who plays Hera in *Star Wars Rebels* was the first cast-member from the show we interviewed for the magazine. In researching her for the interview—something all interviewers should do—I discovered that her mother is Joan Van Ark—TV royalty! She had played Spider-Woman in a short-lived, but very popular animated series. One episode featured Spider-Woman battling what looked suspiciously like Wookiees (the episode was called "A Crime in Time" if you feel like investigating)! On telling Vanessa, midway through the interview, she found the episode on YouTube. There really is no escape from *Star Wars*! Following the interview, we kept in contact, leading to Vanessa writing the Vanessa's View column in the *Insider*.
—Jonathan Wilkins

Vanessa Marshall (born October 19, 1969) is most active in voice-over roles for animated series, films, and videogames. She is the daughter of actress Joan Van Ark and reporter John Marshall. She began voice-over work after being discovered performing a one-woman show. Her roles include Black Widow in Avengers: Earth's Mightiest Heroes, *Mary Jane Watson in* The Spectacular Spider-Man, *and Wonder Woman in* Justice League. *She most recently voiced the role of Gamora in the* Guardians of the Galaxy *animated series.*

HERA
A NEW BREED OF HERO

BEFORE HER PART AS HERA SYNDULLA
IN *STAR WARS REBELS* HAS EVEN AIRED,
ACTRESS VANESSA MARSHALL IS ALREADY
A HUGE HIT WITH FANS! *INSIDER* MET THE
LADY HERSELF FOR A CHAT AHEAD OF THE
SERIES' HOTLY ANTICIPATED DEBUT!
WORDS: JONATHAN WILKINS

Star Wars Insider: You recently appeared at
Star Wars Weekends—you're the queen
of the *Star Wars* selfies—how did it all go?
Vanessa Marshall: I had so much fun; it was epic.
Really, I could not believe the fans' reaction; it was
heaven on earth. Everyone is just so jolly about the whole thing,
and really into it in a way that's so kind and loving. You know,
some are Sith, some are Jedi, but we all get along!

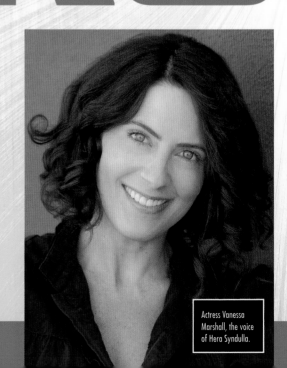

Actress Vanessa
Marshall, the voice
of Hera Syndulla.

Your mom, Joan Van Ark, played the title role in the *Spider-Woman* animated series in the late 1970s. Was that an influence in you doing voice-acting?
Not at all. When I was growing up, my mom was the voice of Estée Lauder and she did a few cartoons, but her career was mostly on camera. I wasn't even aware that she specifically played Spider-Woman until I googled

"WHEN I GOT THE PART OF HERA, I CRIED TEARS OF JOY... IT'S A NERD'S DREAM COME TRUE."

it and discovered that we had a similar background!

I actually fell into voice-acting quite accidentally. I was doing sketch comedy

when an agent discovered me in 1997, and I've been working ever since.

What was the audition process for *Rebels* like?
I got called in for a voiceover audition for a project called "Wolf." I felt like it could be *Star Wars*, but I thought I wouldn't be so fortunate; I thought there were elements of the Rebel Alliance in the text. For example, my character was fighting against the

"Tyranny," and I wondered if that might be the Empire.

I remember saying to my friends, "Do you think this is *Star Wars*?" and they thought I was crazy for even suggesting it. When I got a call back, however, and I saw a picture of a Twi'lek on the wall, I almost passed out! I was right! I drove away thinking, Well, if nothing else happens in my life, getting called back for *Star Wars* is probably the highlight right there! When I got the part, I cried tears of joy. I kept saying, "How'd I get so lucky? How'd I get so lucky?" I am beyond grateful. It's a nerd's dream come true.

Can you tell us about Hera and her place in the show?
Hera is at the heart of the *Ghost* crew. She is both an ace pilot and a skilled fighter. She is the getaway driver, and, while she is a tough cookie, she also manages to be quite nurturing, if not maternal, as she guides and inspires her band of "rebels."

Hera could probably manage alone, but she prefers to fight crime throughout the galaxy with her chosen dysfunctional family. She selected each person for specific reasons. Sabine is a weapons expert and can speak many languages. Kanan is a Jedi, and Ezra is his Padawan. It never hurts to have a couple of Jedi on board! Zeb offers pure might and brawn, while Chopper keeps things running—that little guy can take out a few TIE fighters in a pinch!

Were you given a backstory for Hera?
There were a few things mentioned, but I'm not at liberty to discuss the specifics. I think it's going be really cool for viewers to find out more about each character's backstory. They've all been maligned by the Empire, and we will soon discover their very personal reasons for rebelling against it. The characters themselves will learn these things about each other as the story unfolds, so it's not out in the open... yet.

Dave Filoni is a great ambassador for *Star Wars*, but I wondered what makes him such a good supervising director?
Well, I think it's a number of things.

Hera takes the controls of the *Ghost;* below, a production maquette created to let the *Rebels* team know what the character will look like in 3D.

123

Vanessa greets two young fans at Disney's *Star Wars* Weekends!

The *Ghost*, the rebel ship piloted by Hera Syndulla.

In addition to his familiarity with the saga in its entirety, Dave has a way of trusting the actors to do what they do best. He allows us to do our thing and then comments afterward. What's really cool about Dave is he's from Pittsburgh, plays hockey, likes the Steelers—he's a guy's guy. I really like directors who are perhaps more blunt and just shoot from the hip, because why waste time, really? Dave is wise and chooses his words carefully, and as a result he gets the job done quickly. I also think the way he gathers the cast before each session— almost like we're in a locker room before a big game—helps to focus the group.

We basically get together, and he tells us why this episode's arc is vital

> **"WHEN I SAW THE LITTLE LEGO *STAR WARS* HERA FIGURE... IT WAS THE COOLEST THING EVER!"**

in terms of the next step of the narrative. We huddle up and then we go for it! It's a lot of fun. I think when a cast is having such a good time, the viewers can feel that energy and ultimately they will enjoy the show even more. It all

starts with Dave, igniting that spark for all of us.

Did Hera look exactly how you expected?
No. I thought she would look more like Sigourney Weaver! But I am thrilled that she is a Twi'lek. There's a false perception that Twi'leks are mostly slave dancers. People forget brave characters such as the Jedi Aayla Secura or the courageous Twi'lek fighters in the Ryloth arc of *The Clone Wars* like Cham Syndulla.

It's unfair to generalize, but many of my friends say "Oh you're like the girl who dances for Jabba?" And I say, "No, I'm not."

Will you be saving all the Hera collectibles?
I'm on it, man! When I saw the little LEGO *Star Wars* Hera figure at the Toy Fair in Germany, you should have seen the dance I did! I mean the footwork was exceptional! It was just the coolest thing ever....

MORE TO SAY

Follow Vanessa Marshall on Twitter @vanmarshall

HAVE YOU?

124

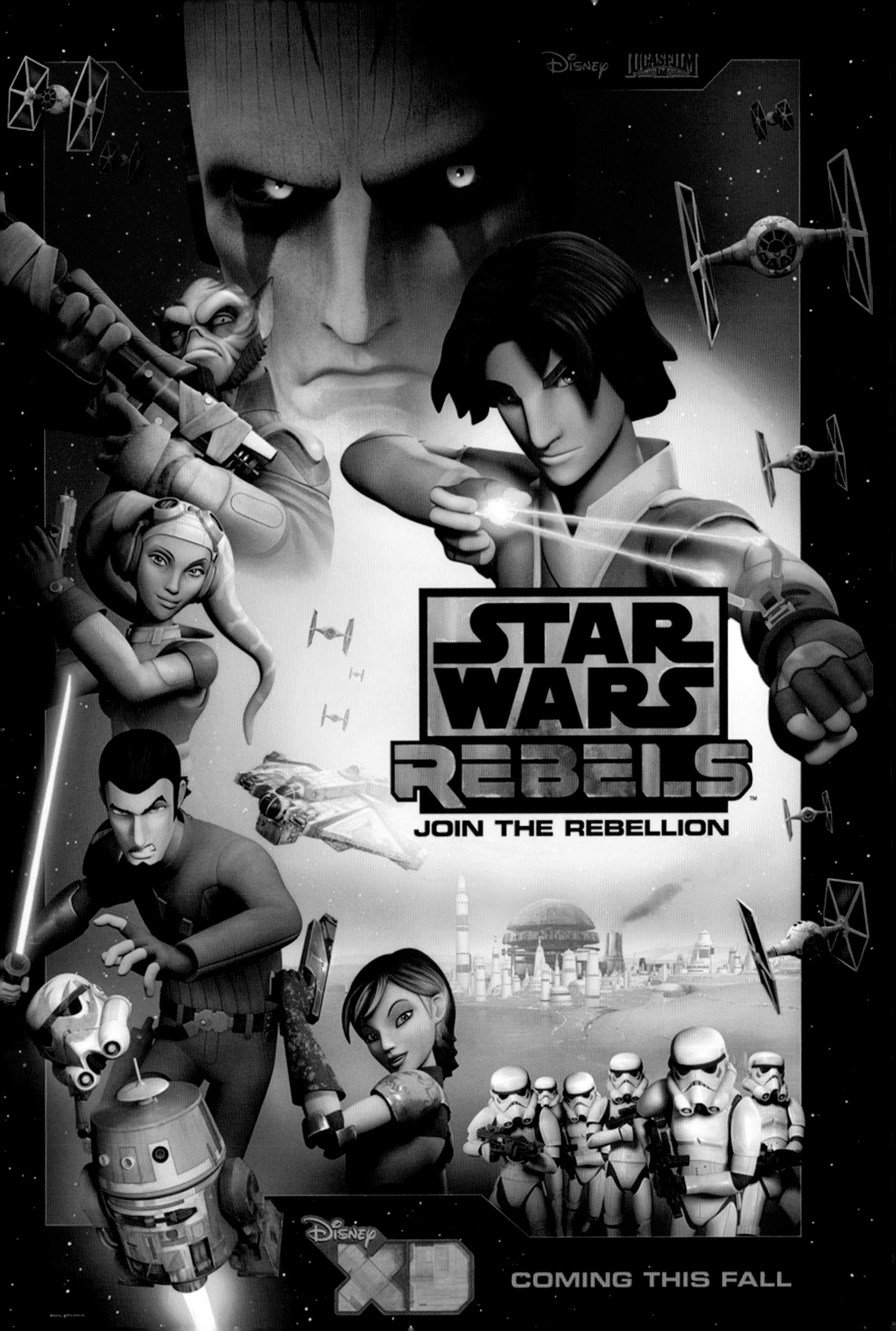
Disney
LUCASFILM
STAR WARS
REBELS™
JOIN THE REBELLION
Disney XD
COMING THIS FALL

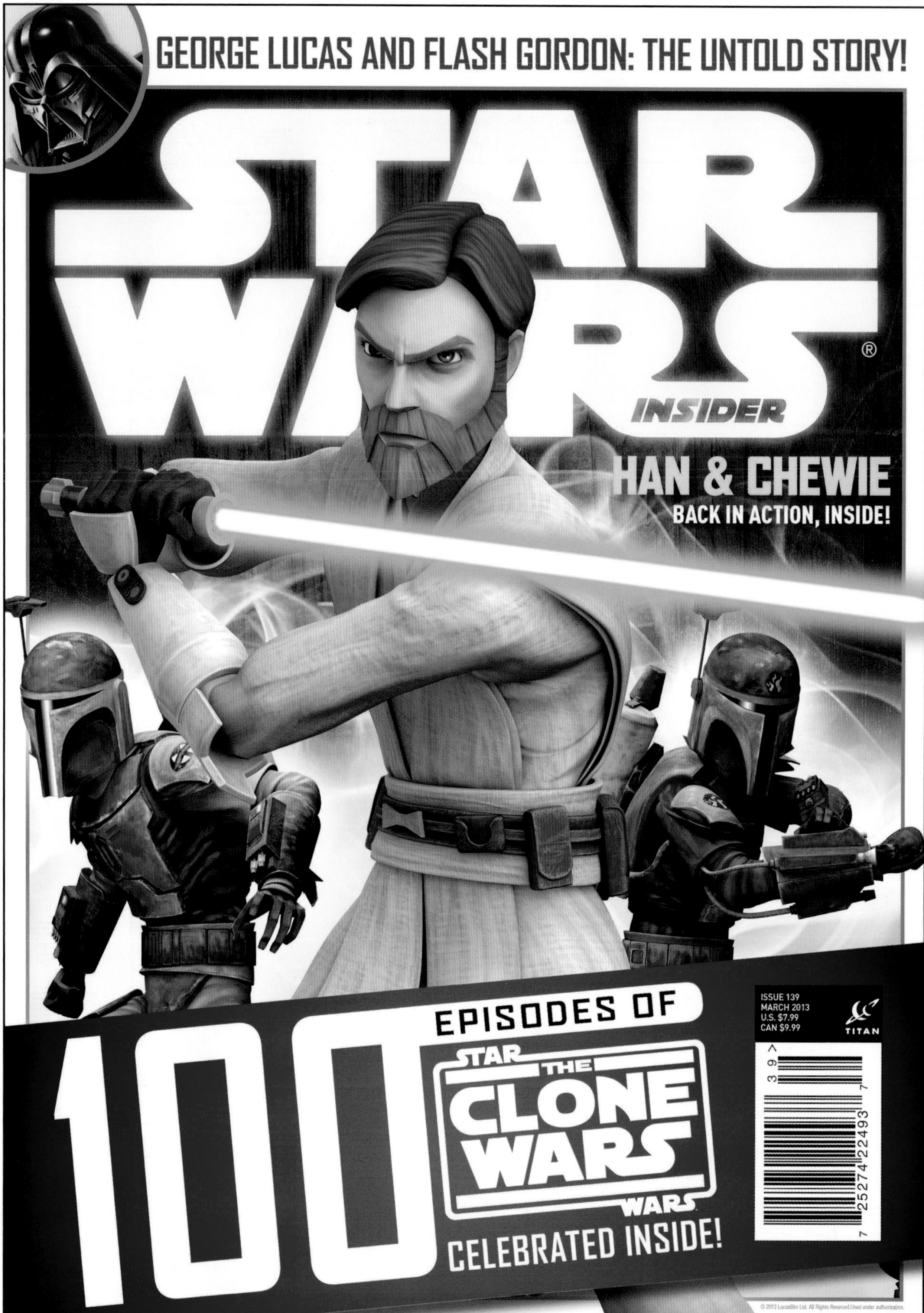

GEORGE LUCAS AND FLASH GORDON: THE UNTOLD STORY!
STAR WARS®
INSIDER
HAN & CHEWIE
BACK IN ACTION, INSIDE!
ISSUE 139
MARCH 2013
U.S. $7.99
CAN $9.99
TITAN
100
EPISODES OF
STAR WARS THE CLONE WARS
CELEBRATED INSIDE!
© 2013 Lucasfilm Ltd. All Rights Reserved. Used under authorization.

BRIAN DALEY
THE HAN SOLO ADVENTURES

ISSUE 139
MARCH 2013

THIS MONTH, FAR, FAR AWAY....

Star Wars: The Clone Wars "The Wrong Jedi" aired on Cartoon Network

Star Wars: Dark Times 24: Fire Carrier, Part 2 released

It is announced that *Star Wars: The Clone Wars* is to end

Star Wars 3: In the Shadow of Yavin, Part 3 released

Star Wars: The Clone Wars: Defenders of the Lost Temple released

Star Wars: Legacy 1: Prisoner of the Floating World, Part 1 released

Star Wars: Dawn of the Jedi: The Prisoner of Bogan 4 released

If there is one person from *Star Wars* history that I would love to have interviewed, it would have to be the late Brian Daley. A writer of immense talent who adapted the original trilogy for radio, Daley also wrote three much-loved novels featuring Han Solo. It's wonderful to be able to pay small, but hopefully significant, tribute to him in *Insider*, and to remind readers of the richness of his work.—**Jonathan Wilkins**

Brian Charles Daley (December 22, 1947–February 11, 1996) was the author of The Han Solo Adventures, *a trilogy of novels detailing Han and Chewbacca's adventures in the Corporate Sector and the Tion Hegemony before they joined the Rebel Alliance. He also wrote radio drama adaptations of the original trilogy. Daley died of pancreatic cancer shortly after the radio dramatization of* Return of the Jedi *finished recording.*

AUTHORS OF THE EXPANDED UNIVERSE
BRIAN DALEY

BY MICHAEL KOGGE

IN THE EVER-EXPANDING LORE OF *STAR WARS*, FEW HAVE CAPTURED ITS CHARACTERS AS WELL AS THE LATE NOVELIST BRIAN DALEY. HIS HAN SOLO BOOKS, PUBLISHED TWO YEARS AFTER THE RELEASE OF *A NEW HOPE*, ARE STILL REGARDED BY MANY READERS AS THE BEST IN THEIR GENRE. HIS RADIO ADAPTATIONS OF THE ORIGINAL FILMS CONTINUE TO ASTOUND LISTENERS WITH THEIR REMARKABLE SCOPE AND DALEY'S GIFT FOR ELEVATING DIALOGUE. AS HIS BEST FRIEND AND FELLOW COLLABORATOR JIM LUCENO ATTESTS, BRIAN DALEY AND *STAR WARS* WERE A PERFECT MARRIAGE OF WRITER AND SUBJECT. IT WAS A MARRIAGE THAT ALMOST DIDN'T HAPPEN....

Ballantine/26166/$1.95

DEL REY

HAN SOLO AT STARS' END

A NOVEL BY BRIAN DALEY

FROM THE ADVENTURES OF LUKE SKYWALKER BASED ON THE CHARACTERS AND SITUATIONS CREATED BY GEORGE LUCAS

Brian Daley, author and scriptwriter.

HAN SOLO'S REVENGE

A NOVEL BY BRIAN DALEY

FROM THE ADVENTURES OF LUKE SKYWALK
BASED ON THE CHARACTERS AND
SITUATIONS CREATED BY GEORGE LUCAS

DEL REY

HAN SOLO AND THE LOST LEGACY™

A NOVEL BY BRIAN DALEY

FROM THE ADVENTURES OF LUKE SKYWALKER,
BASED ON THE CHARACTERS AND
SITUATIONS CREATED BY GEORGE LUCAS

TM: A Trademark of Lucasfilm, Ltd.

Brian Daley at Wit's End

I n 1978, Daley suffered from "the classic second novel curse." Passion had fueled the writing of his first novel, *The Doomfarers of Coramonde*. But its sequel, *The Starfollowers of Coramonde*, proved a difficult slog. His editor, Lester del Rey, demanded exhaustive rewrites, nearly driving the young author to despair. Daley soon realized natural talent alone wouldn't make him the professional writer he dreamed of being. He would have to improve his skills as a storyteller if he wanted to avoid returning to his day job of steam-cleaning UPS trucks. Before he began his next novel, Daley asked his publisher if there was work-for-hire he could take to hone his craft. So, Judy Lynn del Rey, the other half of the Del Rey imprint, offered him the chance to write a *Star Wars* book.

A young Brian Daley relaxes during his college years.

Daley in Central Park with old roommate Jeff Pagano. Pagano's second son, born shortly after Brian's death, was named Daley in memory of Brian.

Rogues, Rebels, and Robots

T he possibility of writing in the galaxy of the biggest blockbuster since *Gone With the Wind* excited Daley no end. He and Luceno had seen the film a year before, walking into a matinee without high expectations, then coming out wanting to watch it again. Daley saw *Star Wars* as a love letter to the science fiction he had read as a boy, from Edgar Rice Burroughs to Robert Heinlein. He knew this universe of rebels and robots like a kid knew his toys. Space opera was a genre he could sing.

Dreaming of mystical warriors and galactic empires, Daley proposed a story about Luke and Leia that explored the history of the Jedi. His novel would be more than just a tie-in, it would truly expand the *Star Wars* universe.

Plans, however, were already in motion for *The Empire Strikes Back*, and Lucasfilm did not want the novels to contradict the film's continuity. Daley was told he could submit another proposal as long as it did not touch on the Jedi, the Force, the Empire, or Darth Vader.

Daley was disheartened. Weren't these the essential ingredients of what made *Star Wars* so special? What was *Star Wars* without its magic or the backdrop of a cosmic civil war?

DALEY SAW *STAR WARS* AS A LOVE LETTER TO THE SCIENCE FICTION HE HAD READ AS A BOY.

Daley and Lucia Robson at Martha's Vineyard.

Daley poses with newlyweds Jim Luceno and Karen Ann Lichten-stein in Annapolis, MD.

Han Solo played a leading role not only in Daley's novels, but also in his sketchbook.

A rare moment of fancy for Daley, who usually wore jeans and T-shirts even to black-tie affairs, like the one thrown in New York City for the NPR series.

Daley donated to a favorite orphanage in Vietnam for many years after he returned home from the war.

The Han Solo Solution

Before he refused the offer, Daley reflected again on the strongest elements of *Star Wars*. He looked beyond the film's mythic archetypes and heard a voice in Lucas' story that spoke to him: Han Solo. "He's the only one who makes a moral decision in the course of the movie that changes him," Daley said on WAMU's *Derek McGinty Show* in 1993. "Everyone else starts out bad and ends up bad, or starts out good and ends up good. He's the one who turns around in the middle of his departure and comes back." A story about the early adventures that had toughened Solo might provide Daley with a fresh hook.

There was another reason that attracted Daley to Solo. Sardonic yet stubborn, with a razor wit and an eye for the ladies, Solo was a character Daley knew quite well. Anyone who had become acquainted with Daley fondly remembers him as the life of any party, a wild and charming guy who always had the best lines and was unafraid of trying any crazy scheme.

"Brian was the Irish version of Han Solo," says Myra DiBlasio, Daley's younger sister.

Jersey Haunts

Brian Charles Daley was born on December 22, 1947, in the middle of a New Jersey snowstorm. His attraction to space came from watching meteor showers with his father, but it was his mother who gave him the reading bug when she handed him a copy of *The Black Stallion* during summer vacation. From that moment on, Daley's nose was in a book, especially Marvel comics and science fiction. Fortune had it that Edgar Snow, the famous author of *Red Star Over China*, lived nearby and used to regale the boy with his globetrotting stories. Soon, Brian had the urge to write. While the other kids played outside, he would be typing away at his great American novel.

Military service was a sacred duty in Daley's Irish-American family. His father and brother had served, and his mother expected Brian to follow in their footsteps. To the 17-year-old Daley, writing now seemed a flight of fancy. The day he enlisted in the U.S. Army to fight in Vietnam, he consigned his magnum opus to the flames. "I do not recall him ever mentioning that he wanted to be a writer," says Edward Elkins, with whom Brian Daley served.

After Vietnam and two years in West Berlin, Daley returned home. Like many soldiers, the war haunted him. Fire alarms triggered flashbacks of artillery fire. Often he would wake up in the middle of the night, shouting from nightmares.

Yet Daley's service to his country also inspired him. While attending Jersey City State College on the G.I. Bill, he began writing again. He started two novels—one serious, the other frivolous. It soon became clear that the frivolous one, about American soldiers in Vietnam who are teleported to a fantastical land, was the better story, giving him an outlet for both his imagination and his military experience.

Fast Friends

While working odd jobs, Daley revised the manuscript of what would become *The Doomfarers of Coramonde*, collecting enough publishers' rejection notes to paper his bathroom. But he carried on rewriting, convinced he would see the novel published. His girlfriend at the time had a friend who was also seeing a writer, so the two set up a double date that sparked Daley's close friendship with James Luceno.

Luceno was blown away when he read Daley's manuscript. "It just seemed to me that he had every word right," Luceno says. The Del Rey editors in New York eventually agreed. On July 6, 1976, Daley received a phone call that changed his life. He had sold his first novel to Del Rey Books and was quickly asked to write a sequel.

"If I could draw a line right through my life... it's that day, that minute, that phone call," Daley said at Jersey City State University in 1990.

> ## "I WANTED LUKE TO BE LIKE A LOT OF SCIENCE FICTION FANS."

Judy – Lynn Del Rey
Ballantine/Del Rey Books
201 East 50th St.
NYC 10022.

Dear Judy – Lynn,

I find, to my great chagrin, that I don't have all the pages for which you requested changes, but I think we can handle this thing anyway. If this doesn't suffice, ring my chime, and we can (or a proofreader and I can) settle it over the phone; regrets for the trouble.

There are two pages still to be changed, as follows:

1½) The other use of "sophantic cultureologist" is on page 23, of which I have none of. The construction may have to be changed a little, to insure that the reader knows the girls are "undergrad students in Non-Human Sociology" and not "Non-Human Sociologists," which is to say a couple of your Alien types.

2.) The other missing page is #42, which so dazzled you with its colorful lines and swirls. To simplify things, the only really vital change for that page (in the interests of your sanity) is addition a of a sentence or two to this effect:

"Police ground-cruisers and aircraft, converging under Traffic Control's direction, were already beginning to gather, further down the highway. Since Chewbacca had elected to leave the road in a unique manner, it would probably take the local authorities some time to piece together what had happened."

. . . even the Wook and Solo can't tear up the landscape without the cops taking some sort of notice.

Glad you liked the book. I understand now why you were unwilling to discuss The Empire Strikes Back; it's quite a hat-trick. See you for St. Pat's Day, if not before. My very best to Lester.

As ever,

Brian Daley

Brian Daley

A letter from Daley offers a peek behind the scenes of the writing process, while corrections from Lucasfilm (opposite page) show how *Han Solo's Revenge* was fine-tuned.

Postproduction supervisor Tom Voegeli, director John Madden, and scriptwriter Daley during the NPR recording of *Star Wars*.

Radio Days

The success of the Han Solo novels opened an unexpected door for Daley. Lucasfilm and NPR hired him to adapt the films into radio plays when the originally contracted writer turned in an unusable draft. (*The Best of Star Wars Insider Volume 3* provides an extensive behind-the-scenes look at the making of the *Star Wars* radio trilogy.) These were some of the best days in Daley's writing life.

Daley bonded with Luke, finding affinity for the Anchorhead misfit in his own boyhood. "I wanted Luke to be like a lot of science fiction fans," Daley said to Topps editor Bob Woods in a 1995 interview. "He knows there's something bigger out there, and that sometimes he doesn't fit in." While the other youths call Luke "Wormie"—a nod to King Arthur's nickname "Wart" in T.H. White's *The Sword in the Stone*—Luke "doesn't accept their judgement. He thinks maybe they're the ones who are wrong."

George Lucas did not have any direct involvement in the radio series, though Daley sent the director a letter after *Star Wars* aired, dying to know his opinion. Lucas wrote back saying he had enjoyed it. "That note meant a lot to me, that he thought I hadn't screwed up his world," Daley told Woods.

Celia Strain 1981

STAR WARS™

EXCLUSIVELY ON PUBLIC RADIO

FROM A GALAXY FAR, FAR AWAY
THE BIGGEST BOX OFFICE HIT IN MOVIE HISTORY IS NOW A STUNNING STEREO RADIO EXPERIENCE
EXCLUSIVELY ON KUSC FM, Los Angeles
LISTEN TO THE ADVENTURES OF LUKE SKYWALKER AS HE AND HIS FRIENDS CONFRONT THE EMPIRE IN 13 EXCITING EPISODES
Star Wars is a production of National Public Radio in association with KUSC FM, Los Angeles, and with the cooperation of Lucasfilm.

Gambler's Choice

Daley's second pitch to Lucasfilm for a Han Solo adventure received their approval. With a deadline of little more than a month, writing this novel became the perfect opportunity to sharpen his craft. Unable to rely on movie lore, Daley created his own pocket universe tailored to Solo, peppering it with high-flying swoops, corporate goons, ancient despots, and deadly war-robots.

The resulting book, which Daley called *The Millennium Falcon Deal* but which was re-titled *Han Solo at Stars' End*, became a *New York Times* bestseller. Straightaway, Del Rey contracted Daley to write two sequels, *Han Solo's Transit* and *Han Solo Collections Ltd.*, which became *Han Solo's Revenge* and *Han Solo and the Lost Legacy*.

Daley's decision to take the *Star Wars* job not only cemented his status as a full-time author, it also led him to the love of his life. In true Solo fashion, he caught the glance of a former Peace Corps volunteer during a screening of trailers at Baltimore sci-fi convention Balticon 13. When the trailer for *Star Wars* played, Daley asked the young lady if she had read the new Han Solo book. "I never read movie spin-offs," scoffed Lucia Robson.

The man sitting next to Daley, Del Rey editor Owen Lock, turned to Robson and revealed that it was Daley who wrote that spin-off. An embarassed Robson promptly bought Daley a drink to apologize. They hit it off immediately and were together for the next 16 years.

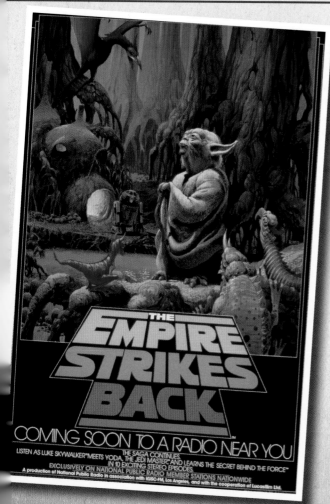

Daley considered the recording of *The Empire Strikes Back* to be one of most fulfilling times of his career. Photo: John Bos.

The Secret Life of Jack McKinney

After NPR's *The Empire Strikes Back* was broadcast in 1983, funding for NPR's dramas had dried up, so an adaptation of *Jedi* did not seem possible. Daley wrote the script for a short audio drama, *Rebel Mission to Ord Mantell*, and outlined an episode of the *Droids* cartoon that was never produced. With popular interest in *Star Wars* waning, Daley worked on his own novels, scripted the animated series *Galaxy Rangers*, and, under the pseudonym of Jack McKinney teamed with Luceno to pen more than 20 *Robotech* books.

Still, Daley longed to return to the galaxy far, far away. When the *Star Wars* fiction license came up for renewal at Del Rey in 1989, Daley and Luceno proposed a new series that would recount Luke re-establishing the Jedi Order. Lucasfilm, however, granted Bantam Books the license. Since he was not part of Bantam's stable of authors, Daley pushed ahead on his epic *GammaLAW* series.

BRIAN DALEY SELECT BIBLIOGRAPHY

The Doomfarers of Coramonde (1977)

The Starfollowers of Coramonde (1979)

The Han Solo Adventures: Han Solo at Stars' End; Han Solo's Revenge, Han Solo and the Lost Legacy (1979, 1979, 1980)

Star Wars Trilogy (National Public Radio Dramatizations 1981, 1983, 1996)

TRON (novelization, 1982)

A Tapestry of Magics (1983)

Star Wars: Rebel Mission to Ord Mantell (audio drama LP/cassette 1983)

The Adventures of Hobart Floyt and Alacrity Fitzhugh: Requiem for a Ruler of Worlds; Jinx on a Terran Inheritance; Fall of the White Ship Avatar (1985, 1985, 1986)

The Adventures of the Galaxy Rangers (animated series 1986)

GammaLAW: Smoke on the Water, Screaming Across the Sky; The Broken Country, To Water's End (1997, 1998, 1998, 1999)

A wee Brian (center) with his dad, Charles, and big brother, David.

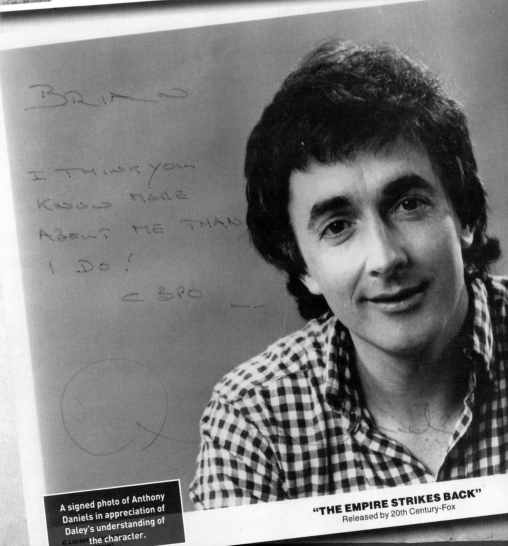

A signed photo of Anthony Daniels in appreciation of Daley's understanding of the character.

BRIAN

I THINK YOU KNOW MORE ABOUT ME THAN I DO!

C 3PO

"THE EMPIRE STRIKES BACK"
Released by 20th Century-Fox

134

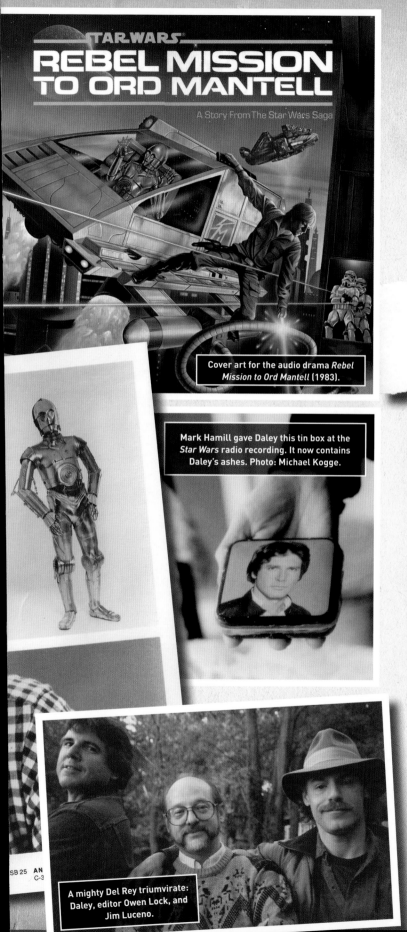

STAR WARS
REBEL MISSION TO ORD MANTELL

A Story From The Star Wars Saga

Cover art for the audio drama *Rebel Mission to Ord Mantell* (1983).

Mark Hamill gave Daley this tin box at the *Star Wars* radio recording. It now contains Daley's ashes. Photo: Michael Kogge.

A mighty Del Rey triumvirate: Daley, editor Owen Lock, and Jim Luceno.

Circle of the Force

I n 1995, Daley was still working on *GammaLAW* when he was called back to *Star Wars*. Highbridge Audio, the publishers of the radio drama on tape and CD, wanted to finish the trilogy with a *Return of the Jedi* radio adaptation. Though few people knew, Daley was suffering from pancreatic cancer, the same illness that had killed his boyhood idol, Edgar Snow.

Daley poured himself into the scripts, even as his cancer worsened. He put everything else aside, including *GammaLAW*, for this chance to complete his *Star Wars* trilogy. Sadly, he never heard his lines broadcast. Brian Daley died on February 11, 1996, the night the cast finished recording *Jedi* in Los Angeles.

> ANTHONY DANIELS BELIEVED BRIAN DALEY TO BE THE ONE WRITER WHO TRULY CAPTURED C-3PO'S VOICE.

Blood of a Jedi

D aley's loss touched many in the *Star Wars* community. Some fans claim to have felt "a disturbance in the Force" at his passing. Both Anthony Daniels and Dark Horse editor Ryder Windham, with whom Daley planned to collaborate on a *Droids* comic, were devastated. Daniels believed Daley to be the one writer who truly captured C-3PO's voice, often giving the golden droid scene-stealing lines.

Jeffrey Pagano, Brian's roommate when he wrote the Solo books, perhaps best summarizes the sentiments to Daley and his writing: "I always knew that whatever he was working on (from *Star Wars* to the novelization for *TRON* to *GammaLAW*) involved the struggle to achieve justice, whether rough or otherwise. His work is and will be remembered in my view, because he focused upon the fundamental human struggle to always do the right thing."

As a writer, Brian Daley mirrored his muse Han Solo in more ways than one. ☻

EXPANDED

MICHAEL KOGGE most recently wrote "Gentleman of Virginia" for *A Princess of Mars—The Annotated Edition*—and *New Tales of the Red Planet* (Sword & Planet Press).

UNIVERSE

Many thanks to Lucia Robson, Jim Luceno, Lindsey Loeper, Bob Woods, Pablo Hidalgo, Owen Lock, Robert Booker, Edward Elkins, Ryder Windham, and Jeffrey Pagano.

FEATURING GUEST EDITOR WARWICK DAVIS!

STAR WARS ®

INSIDER

CELEBRATING 30 YEARS OF

RETURN

OF THE

JEDI

With
MARK HAMILL
ANTHONY DANIELS
AND MORE

TITAN

ISSUE 143
AUGUST/
SEPTEMBER
2013

U.S. $7.99
CAN $9.99

PLUS: EXCLUSIVE FICTION! ● ALL-NEW COLLECTIBLES! ● RARE PHOTOS! ● EWOKS!

LUKE SKYWALKER
MARK HAMILL

ISSUE 143
AUGUST/SEPTEMBER 2013

THIS MONTH, FAR, FAR AWAY....

Star Wars 8 released

Star Wars: Dark Times 29: A Spark Remains, Part 2 released

Star Wars: Darth Vader and the Ninth Assassin 5 released

Gilbert Taylor (cinematographer) dies, aged 99

Star Wars: Kenobi released

Star Wars: Jedi Academy released

The Star Wars 1 released

Star Wars 9 released

Star Wars: Dark Times 30: A Spark Remains, Part 3 released

Angry Birds *Star Wars* II released

Empire and Rebellion: Razor's Edge released

Star Wars: Legacy Volume 27 released

While I have enjoyed interviewing all manner of *Star Wars* cast, crew, and creators, this interview with Mark Hamill remains my favorite. Luke Skywalker was my hero growing up and remains so to this day.

When I was a seven-year-old kid, I saved my allowance so that I could afford to see him in *Amadeus* on Broadway—to no avail as, well, I was a seven-year-old kid living in southern England.

The interview was conducted via telephone at 3am in the U.K. I have never felt so nervous. Thankfully, all nerves were soon dissolved by the sheer good nature of the interview. Hamill is a delightful subject, chatting away in his iconic Joker voice prior to the interview before discussing his relationship with *Star Wars* fans—boy, does he love and appreciate his fans —and, of course, the movies themselves. They say never meet your heroes— or telephone them—but I'm still thrilled to have been given the opportunity to speak with a true legend of the *Star Wars* saga.—**Jonathan Wilkins**

Mark Richard Hamill (born September 25, 1951) is best known for portraying Luke Skywalker in the original Star Wars *trilogy (1977-1983), a role he reprised in* Star Wars: The Force Awakens *(2015). Hamill has forged a successful career as a voice actor, most notably supplying a fan-favorite performance as the Joker in the Batman franchise, beginning with* Batman: The Animated Series *in 1992.*

JOURNEY TO JEDI

THIRTY-SIX YEARS AFTER WE FIRST INVESTED IN LUKE SKYWALKER'S EPIC JOURNEY FROM WHINING FARMBOY TO FEARLESS JEDI, ACTOR MARK HAMILL IS STILL IN AWE OF THE PASSION OF *STAR WARS* FANS. IN THIS EXCLUSIVE INTERVIEW, HAMILL CHATS ABOUT FILMING THE TRILOGY, AND RECALLS HIS GRADUAL REALIZATION THAT NOTHING WOULD EVER BE THE SAME AGAIN. INTERVIEW BY JONATHAN WILKINS

Star Wars Insider: Can you remember what your first thoughts were when you read the *Star Wars* script?
Mark Hamill: One thing I thought was, *This thing is hilarious!* Most science fiction is very dry, but the dialogue in *Star Wars* was so funny. This idea of robots arguing over whose fault it is... [C-3PO impersonation]: "I've forgotten how much I abhor space travel!" I was just falling out of my chair laughing! The robots are so human and warm.

I also loved the character of Han Solo. I thought it was so smart to have a cynical, modern day voice mocking the Force. He really doesn't care one way or the other: He's in it for the money. I thought, *That's really going to draw a lot of people in who would resist this kind of material, because they'll completely identify with him.* I knew Harrison Ford's work from *American Graffiti*. I thought, *Oh, this guy's just going to knock it out of the ballpark*—and of course, he did!

There's also a spirituality there that was unusual for science-fiction. They were talking about this entity that's bigger than all of us, that links us together... It was pretty heavy stuff for the kind of Saturday matinee, fun serial, which it was emulating.

Did you spend much time working with Sir Alec Guinness?
I got a chance to get to know him and I asked him outright, "Why did you want to do this?" He was so legendary in his accomplishments, and I was so flattered to be in something that he thought was worthy for his résumé! He said to me [Sir Alec Guinness impersonation], "Well, I've always wanted to play a wizard..."

He saw—very much like I did—that it was more like a fairytale than traditional science-fiction. Science-fiction tends to be a projection of what life will be in the future from the point of view of Earthlings—and fantasy can be anything! There's a big furry ape-like creature flying your spaceship, wearing headphones, not wearing any pants? Sure, why not? It's fantasy!

The films combine elements of so many wonderful things: from the Ray Harryhausen films, to *The Wizard of Oz*, to *Captain Blood*, to *The Searchers*. It's a movie-lover's dream to work in something that plays on so many elements that make cinema unique.

How much information did George Lucas give you about the character and the wider story?
I was so enamored of the material when I was doing those films that I was peppering George with questions all the time. All that extraneous minutiae that fans revel in was just dripping from every pore in my body. What planet does a Wookiee come from? Where did Chewbacca learn how to fly a starship? And I remember asking George, "Why am I living with my aunt and uncle?

"ALEC GUINNESS SAID TO ME, 'WELL, I'VE ALWAYS WANTED TO PLAY A WIZARD...'"

Main image: Luke faces down Jabba the Hutt in an effort to rescue his friends — an iconic still from *Return of the Jedi*!

Left: Toasting Sir Alec Guinness on the Mos Eisley set during Guinness's birthday celebration on location for the first *Star Wars*.

Left, below: A prisoner of Jabba, but still defiant!

Right: A moment of contemplation from George Lucas, Sir Alec Guinness, and Hamill as they shoot Obi-Wan and Luke's first fateful meeting.

Below: An iconic shot of Luke Skywalker, Jedi Knight!

MARK HAMILL ON *STAR WARS'* RUNNING TIME

While we were making the first *Star Wars* movie, I asked George how long it was going to be. He said, "Hmmm, maybe an hour and 57 minutes." That was just like George to say something that specific! He said, "Anything over two-hours is an epic!" His thinking has changed over the years, obviously, but he's got a lot more story to tell.

It was never lost on me—that anything over two hours is an epic, and that should give you some idea of at least the approach that we had in those days. You may be an epic, but don't *act* like one. Be true to the material, don't be pretentious and don't be pompous. It was the only way we could do it because it wasn't a foregone conclusion that so many people would have such reverence for it.

It was very loose and ragged around the edges, which I think works well in contrast to the spectacular special effects. I like that kind of knockabout feel that we had.

Obviously, as it went on, we had bigger budgets and the special effects get more and more accomplished. Each movie has a different sort of atmosphere and tone, but we never forgot where we came from.

What happened to my mom and dad?" And, at least in the first film, he actually made up lies, because he couldn't really tell me what was in store! There's got to be an amount of security so big story points don't leak out.

Did you think the film was going to be as big as it was?
When I first met the production manager, Robert Watts, he said "What do you think of this script and this movie?" And I said, "I think we're on to a winner. This is going to be bigger than *Planet of the Apes*!" The reason I brought up *Planet of the Apes* was that we'd signed a contract that if the first one was a hit, that it would be a trilogy, with a beginning, a middle, and an end. He was amazed that I was so confident and I said, "Look, even if this thing stumbles at the box office, it will get the reputation of a cult movie, like *The Rocky Horror Picture Show*. It'll be embraced by a small fanbase, and there'll be midnight showings."

Since the first one only cost about $9 million, I figured if we made $25 million, it'll break even. I looked at all the grosses for fantasy/science-fiction since the start of the talkies. I said, "I bet this thing could make upwards of $50 million!" I had no idea we'd be on the cover of *Time* magazine!

What was the atmosphere like during shooting?
We were always reminded that it was a children's film. The British crew could only relate it to something like *Doctor Who* or *Dan Dare* or the more idiosyncratic British things they'd done. They were sure that it would only play at matinees for kids at weekends. I wasn't insulted by that at all! I thought, *They could be right!* What appealed to me was it was also meant for the kid in all of us, much like the Disney films are. You can be moved by *Bambi* or delighted by *Pinocchio* no matter what your age is. It seemed to me that it had great potential.

George isn't the happiest guy when he's directing. In fact he seems sort of morose and depressed! It must be hard because he'd imagined *Star Wars* for so many years and then when you see it realized in a literal sense on set, he was disappointed. "*This* is a lightsaber? It doesn't look so hot!"

Sometimes robots don't exactly behave in the way you want them to—not Anthony Daniels, of course—but the mechanical ones that were meant to do this and that!

We really had to move along. George called it the most expensive low-budget movie ever made, because we didn't have the luxury of infinite takes or expanding our schedule. There was a point where Fox had to consider whether they were going to pull the plug on it because none of the effects had been finished.

It was dodgy for a while. I was on a need-to-know basis, but I learned later that they screened it for Fox executives and George's film buddies with no score—I think they used the classical piece *The Planets* to stand in for what would become John Williams' score. We came dangerously close to becoming one of those movies that is *never* finished. But [Fox President] Alan Ladd and the powers-that-be saw the potential...

So, we nearly didn't have *Star Wars*—and where would we all be then?
I certainly wouldn't be talking to you right now! People don't realize how monumental it was for all of us. It's like being in the eye of a hurricane. It soon took on a life of its own. The day it opened, I went to dub the 35mm print: That's how close to the edge they were playing it!

They'd just finished the 70mm print to get into Grauman's Chinese [movie theater], and when the driver came to pick me up on the day it opened, I said, "Can you go by Grauman's Chinese?" I just wanted to see what it was like out on the marquee. They didn't have a poster! They couldn't agree on a poster for it, so they had just stapled lobby cards outside with no poster. They didn't really know how to promote it: *Is it serious, is it a comedy, what is this?*

MARK HAMILL ON CELEBRATION

Appearing at Celebration is almost like what it must have been like in The Beatles or, more appropriately, The Monkees. Our experience was being chosen by George, rather than organically forming a group like The Beatles. Mickey Dolenz and I will be on lunchboxes as long as we live! We're part of that little niche pop-culture experience that has brought so many people so much pleasure long after we thought it would be all finished.

Opposite page, far left: This seems familiar! Hamill and Carrie Fisher get back in the swing of things!

Main: Luke is captured on Endor as his destiny takes a dangerous turn.

From above: Hamill and Anthony Daniels (C-3PO) share a moment on location; Hamill tries to sweet-talk the skiff guards; Hamill or Hamlet?

"WE LANDED IN CHICAGO FOR A PROMOTIONAL JUNKET, AND THERE WERE ALL THESE PEOPLE AT THE AIRPORT. IT WAS LIKE A MOB SCENE. I SAID TO HARRISON AND CARRIE, 'THERE'S SOMEBODY FAMOUS ON THIS PLANE!'"

There was a line across the block on the very first day! To a certain extent, you know the hardcore fantasy fans are going to be there no matter what—but I remember thinking, *Boy, how's anybody going to know about this thing?*

How did you first come to realize how iconic the movie was becoming?
We landed in Chicago for a promotional junket, and there were all these people at the airport. It was like a mob scene. I said, "There's somebody famous on this plane!" We were looking around, trying to figure it out, thinking it's maybe Teddy Kennedy... As we taxied in, I went, "Carrie, look—there's somebody that has your furry headphones! Look, Harrison—there's a guy with a vest on that looks like you!" And there were people dressed as me, and people with signs saying 'May The Force Be With You.' We were stunned, because it had happened before we could get our minds around it.

Then we never looked back! We were the toast of Chicago; people were inviting us to go to nightclubs and hip places, and we met rock stars! I was relieved, because I thought word-of-mouth would always be our strong point.

The fans discovered *Star Wars* and made it their own, and to a certain extent, the relationship has never changed—it's really bigger than all of us.

Where was the weirdest place you've been recognized?
When I went on my honeymoon with my wife, Marilou, we picked Tahiti because we thought it's like the islands where they filmed *Mutiny on the Bounty*, and it's the closest to paradise on Earth.

There's no television, we didn't listen to the radio... We were like Adam and Eve—back to nature, living in a little hut built over the water. One day I was on the back porch, and I saw a boat on the horizon coming towards me. As it got closer, I saw it was a speedboat, and driving the boat was a man in a Darth Vader mask. I thought briefly that I was hallucinating. I said, "Marilou! Get out here! You're not going to believe this!"

The guy pulled up, dropped anchor, and pulls of the mask. He was laughing his head off. It turned out that he knew Brian Gibbs, who was the accountant on *Star Wars*. He said, "You know Brian from *Star Wars*—the guy who gave out the checks? Well, he's here doing a movie for Dino De Laurentiis." He'd found out that we were staying there! We later saw him at dinner and he said, "I hope you weren't too cross with me, because I thought it would be a funny thing to do."

After that, there's no place you can go to avoid *Star Wars*!

Did you ever want to escape *Star Wars*?
At some point I figured, "I've got to let it go!" Especially when George made the prequels. I didn't know he was going to wait so long to do them! I was drawn to wanting to visit the set, but I thought I should hold back because it should be a fresh start. It should stand on its own. If the roles were reversed, I wouldn't want somebody saying, "Well, in my day we did X, Y, Z."

I didn't want people to think I was trying to give advice or anything. But I did get a really nice telegram from Frank Oz on the very first day of Episode I saying, "It won't be the same without you."

How did you find working with Frank Oz?
I adored Yoda. Frank is so instrumental in that character being what he is—manipulating the figure itself and providing the voice. I remember someone saying, "Does he sound too much like Grover from *Sesame Street*?" And I thought *No, you can't change that voice: It's got to be Frank!*

I never had to make any sort of leap into believing in Yoda. We went on a weekend to rehearse on a non-shooting day, and Frank had to get used to this puppet that [makeup artist] Stuart Freeborn had built with the help of Jim Henson's team. It was the first time we were actually doing scenes together. I'm telling you, the minute he put his hand inside that face, Frank melted away, and to me he was Yoda.

Frank was always very complimentary to me. He said, "Well, if you didn't believe it, then nobody else would believe it."

MARK HAMILL ON GEORGE LUCAS' LEGACY

It's truly an amazing accomplishment for him to have created something that has endured and will continue to endure. It's like L. Frank Baum with the *Oz* books, J.R.R. Tolkien with *Lord of the Rings*, and Gene Roddenberry with *Star Trek*. As long as people have imaginations and the desire to dream and want to enjoy entertainment that takes them out of their everyday lives, then *Star Wars* will never die.

Opposite page: A behind-the-scenes shot of the Yoda puppet and Hamill from *The Empire Strikes Back.*

Left: Working with bluescreen effects was not a problem for Hamill thanks to his strong imagination.

Below: A pause from the action on the Ewok village set during *Return of the Jedi.*

But he was just being modest because [Yoda] wasn't a puppet—he was a real, breathing character.

I think ignorance is bliss because it didn't occur to me that anybody else wouldn't believe in Yoda either, even though it should have. Since he was walking like a Muppet, you never see his feet! One of the most brilliant things is when you see him put one knee up on a box as he's about to climb up, and it cuts to me saying, "Will you get out of there?", not knowing that he's this great Jedi warrior and thinking he's just some eccentric little amphibian. The audience sees that knee go up and the suggestion of his feet is enough so that they fill it in for themselves. That was the only thing I was worried about—that you can't really show him below the waist.

It's the combination of the artistry of Frank Oz and the writing of Lawrence Kasdan—all of it worked.

Was it tough being the only human character on set?
After Carrison—that's what I call Harrison Ford and Carrie Fisher—went back to the United States, I was the only human being

on the call sheet for weeks! It was me, snakes, robots, and a puppet. It got very lonely because Frank, Wendy [Midener, who worked on the Yoda puppet] and all the Yoda operators were below the set. I had an earpiece so that I could hear Frank, but it was not really like being with him. I'd see him at lunch and in the little room where they would run off to repair Yoda when he broke down.

Whenever you see me by myself, I'm not looking at Yoda off-camera. I'm looking at a stick with a piece of tape on it for an eyeline. There were so many problems because there was movement in his ears, and mechanical movement in his eyes. There were problems with Yoda breaking down or looking cross-eyed or the ears not working.

Was working with all the special effects difficult?
Pretend is pretend; I had an overall view of what it looked like in my imagination. People ask, "Was it hard being in something like that where nothing's there or you're working with greenscreen?" Well, I do movies where I'm supposed to be driving a car, and it's a cutaway car in the studio and the crew is rocking the vehicle slightly to make it look like there's movement and they're running lights past my face. How is that any different? It's so unlike really driving a car! And that's not that much different to doing something like being in the cockpit of the *Millennium Falcon* and having them rock that. It's all about pretend. I used to play in the backyard as Zorro or Robin Hood or Sinbad battling skeletons in my mind. That was all the stuff I loved. To this day, I'm so grateful of all

those things that I really loved as a child—whether it's comic books, or movies, or television, or comic strips, or puppets.

I can't put into words how grateful I am for the career I've had. People say, "Oh, it must be terrible. You're so associated with that one thing that you can't be thought of in any other way." I guess there are elements to that, but they're so outweighed by the positives.

Do you ever revisit the *Star Wars* films?
The fact that it's lasted so long is just mind-boggling to me. I feel bad because I haven't seen these movies since they were originally in the movie theaters. It's just not something I do—like, *Hey, let's watch my old TV series or let's watch* The Big Red One [Samuel Fuller's 1980 war epic starring Lee Marvin and Hamill] or whatever. It's not something that I would ordinarily do. ☻

WORLD EXCLUSIVE: *STAR WARS REBELS* LAUNCH ISSUE!

STAR WARS
INSIDER

EXCLUSIVE!
A NEW DAWN
Creating the Stunning
Rebels Prequel Novel!

DROID DESIGN!
Meet the Man who
Builds Real-life Droids!

ISSUE #152
US $7.99
CAN $9.99
OCTOBER 2014

Titan

STAR WARS REBELS

MEET THE CREW OF THE *GHOST*!
THE REBELS: INTERVIEWED INSIDE!
SECRETS OF THE SHOW REVEALED!

7 25274 22493 7

5 2

SABINE WREN
TIYA SIRCAR

ISSUE 152
OCTOBER 2014

Every so often there comes a character that attains a level of popularity that exceeds all expectations. Tiya Sircar's performance as Sabine Wren, a sassy Mandalorian, is one of the highlights of *Star Wars Rebels*. Tiya herself is a delight, extremely funny, and with a genuine knowledge of the saga. As with *Star Wars: The Clone Wars*, Dave Filoni has gathered together a great cast that works as a team. Long may they continue to rebel against the Empire!—**Jonathan Wilkins**

Tiya Sircar (born May 16, 1982) is best known for her roles in The Internship, 17 Again, *and* The Vampire Diaries. *She has also appeared in a wide variety of television shows such as* House M.D., Hannah Montana, Greek, Moonlight, Numbers, Privileged, *and* Terminator: The Sarah Connor Chronicles.

THIS MONTH, FAR, FAR AWAY....

Star Wars Volume 3: Rebel Girl released

Star Wars: Darth Maul—Son of Dathomir trade paperback released

Star Wars Rebels "Spark of Rebellion," "Droids in Distress," "Fighter Flight," and "Rise of the Old Masters" aired Disney XD

Star Wars Rebels: Rebel Journal by Ezra Bridger released

Star Wars: The Adventures of Luke Skywalker, Jedi Knight released

Star Wars Rebels Story and Activity Book released

Star Wars Rebels 3D Activity Book released

Star Wars: The Old Republic: Galactic Strongholds released

Star Wars Art: Posters released

Star Wars Volume 4: A Shattered Hope released

Star Wars Rebels: Ezra's Wookiee Rescue released

Star Wars Costumes: The Original Trilogy released

William Shakespeare's Star Wars Trilogy: The Royal Box Set released

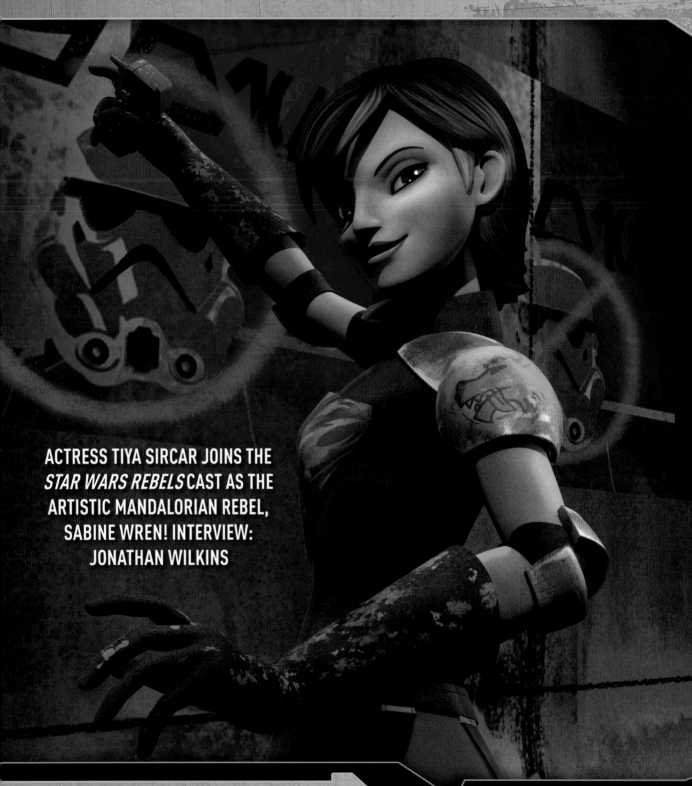

ACTRESS TIYA SIRCAR JOINS THE
STAR WARS REBELS CAST AS THE
ARTISTIC MANDALORIAN REBEL,
SABINE WREN! INTERVIEW:
JONATHAN WILKINS

Star Wars Insider: **This seems like a very different project for you. Is that what attracted you to audition for the show?**
Tiya Sircar: You would be absolutely right, in that it's voiceover and I have a lot more experience doing on-camera acting. The whole science-fiction genre, and specifically *Star Wars*, is a whole new world to me; I've never done anything like it. It's really exciting.

When I auditioned for the show, I actually had no idea it was *Star Wars*. It had a codename, which was "Wolf." So I got a call to audition for what I thought was a new Disney animated series. I didn't actually know it was *Star Wars* until I got the call that I got the job. So it was doubly exciting, like: *Yay I got the job* and then, *Oh my god, it's* Star Wars!

> **"I DIDN'T KNOW I WAS DOING *STAR WARS* UNTIL I GOT THE CALL THAT I GOT THE JOB!"**

And you're not allowed to tell anyone when you're doing *Star Wars*?
We had actually been recording full episodes for quite a while before anyone knew that there was a new *Star Wars* animated series happening, so it was very top secret. I couldn't tell any of my friends or family; it was frustrating but super-exciting! I couldn't share the news with anyone, until I got the OK from Disney and Lucasfilm.

Now that they know that I'm voicing a new *Star Wars* character, many of my friends are coming out of the woodwork as *Star Wars* fans!

Were you a Star Wars fan when you got the part?
I had seen the original *Star Wars* trilogy as a kid, and I was a fan. I knew that it was really special, but I think I was too young to fully appreciate it. Since then, I've gone back and watched the original trilogy and now I totally now get what the fuss is

about. I've been binge-watching episodes of *The Clone Wars* now that they're on Netflix; not only because Dave Filoni is my boss—it's good to do my homework—but I just want to soak up as much *Star Wars* as I can now that I'm part of the universe.

What can you tell us about Sabine?
Well, she's Mandalorian, which is the most recognizable thing about her. As you might figure, she's an expert in combat and weaponry and an explosives expert! She loves to blow things up and she's really good at it.

But I think what sets her apart is that she's a warrior but also she's an artist—a graffiti artist. So it's fitting that she's really anti-establishment, she tags things. I think that's a really cool, special thing about her. Not only does she blow things up, she does it with flair and panache. She leaves these little tagged signatures anytime the *Ghost* crew attack the Empire. She's a teenager with a strong, no-nonsense attitude.

Is she anything like you?
She's awesome, so I hope I'm a little bit like her! I love smart, strong female characters, and I love that I get to portray a teenage girl who isn't interested in superficial stuff; she's got a good head on her shoulders, she's very sharp and quick-witted. So I would love to think we have a little bit in common, but she's more of a kick-butt kind of character than I am. I've never blown anything up, nor have I ever tagged anything, but I live vicariously through Sabine!

Star Wars has this huge female fanbase; it seems just as popular with the girls as guys. Why do you think this is?
I don't see why girls shouldn't be interested in all the action *Star Wars* has to offer, and the science-fiction aspect of it. I can't think of a reason why girls wouldn't be just as interested in it as guys, and I love that Princess Leia is iconic, and Ahsoka is this incredible female character; she's strong and she's a Jedi—and who wouldn't want to be a Jedi?

What I think is really cool about *Rebels* is that these two new female characters

> "I'VE NEVER BLOWN ANYTHING UP OR TAGGED ANYTHING, BUT I LIVE VICARIOUSLY THROUGH SABINE!"

are going to be introduced to the *Star Wars* universe, and they're so different from each other, but they're both, I think, really intelligent and strong women: Hera is this wonderful character—she's nurturing, but she goes out there and attacks the Empire just as fiercely as Kanan or Zeb, or whoever else; and Sabine is an interesting character as well. So I hope that female *Star Wars* fans will appreciate these two new characters. Even though the show hasn't come out, I've already got messages from female fans saying "Oh my gosh, I can't wait for

Sabine," and "I'm already working on my Halloween costume" and all kinds of stuff. So the outpouring of support from *Star Wars* fans in general, but especially female fans, has been overwhelming and amazing.

The Rebels cast have already been embraced by the fans—what do you make of that?
It was incredible, beyond my wildest imagination. Dave Filoni told me "this is what it's going to be like, prepare yourself", but there's no preparing yourself for your first *Star Wars* Weekends. And yeah, it was so special and no-one's even seen the

show yet, and yet we had autograph-signings and people who had drawn pictures of our characters, it was wonderful; and so much fun to meet these incredible people and to have a connection to those people already. I've been receiving tweets in Mando, which I'm trying to learn so I can translate these tweets that I'm getting. My *Star Wars* weekend was so much fun, I hope to do it again. The enthusiasm the fans were showing for a show they haven't even seen yet was amazing, I appreciate it so much. And now I just want people to see the show!

What has been the biggest surprise working on the show?
I think the history, and how deep and rich the mythology is, because, you know, I'm not like Freddie Prinze Jnr. [Kanan] who knows every detail of the *Star Wars* universe. And learning all of it now, being exposed to it now, the Legends and all kinds of things I wasn't familiar with before, it's just been such a learning experience that I'm trying to soak up as much as I can. Growing up, I was a big fan of Greek and Roman mythology, and this is right in line with that, learning about all these incredible characters and their relationships and their stories and the different time periods. It's a lot but I love it, so I'm all in it!

What are the challenges of voice-acting compared to doing live-action work?
It's funny because Taylor Gray [Ezra] and I have a lot more experience doing on-camera acting instead of voice over. You've got Vanessa Marshall [Hera] and Steve Blum [Zeb], who have done nearly only voiceover work, then Freddie's somewhere in the middle—he does it all! Vanessa will be like, "How do you guys do the on-camera stuff—it's so weird!" Taylor and I are like, "How do you do all these crazy voices?"

In a lot of voiceover work, you do your acting in the sound booth by yourself, then you leave and that's that. We get to do something really great, which I think *The Clone Wars* got to do as well. We record all of our episodes together as a group. It's special because we're actually acting these scenes live, in person, and I think that really enriches the entire experience; it makes for better scenes, and better dialogue between the characters.

I've done other work where the animation is finished, and I just come in and do the voice to match what I see. We get to do it the other way around, which is so cool because they record video

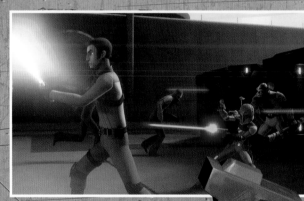

of us acting together in the booth and then send the videos of our recording sessions to the animators. The animators actually use our facial expressions to inform the characters.

It's great because I'm watching Hera and she looks an awful lot like Vanessa even though she's green and has lekku on her head. Each of the characters are eerily similar to the voice actors. I guess that's surprising as well, seeing how much like us they really are. It's a little disconcerting at first, but in the coolest way!

What makes a good voice-director?
Dave Filoni knows everything about *Star Wars*, so that helps! He's been doing this for a long time, but his enthusiasm and zeal for creating these stories has not diminished. He knows all the nuances and all the things that made *The Clone Wars* a success, and hopefully will make *Rebels* as popular. He's so fun to work with; he makes it such a safe environment to try something out. It's a really supportive environment. And if you don't know something, he knows the answer!

Did Sabine look like what you'd envisioned?
We had actually seen the mock-ups of our

characters; I knew what she looked like, but I had never seen her animated.

How does it feel to be immortalized as an action figure?
It's so awesome! The two female characters were revealed at San Diego Comic-Con International this year. I haven't fully processed it yet, so I am beyond excited!

I'm such a big fan of my character, I'm so proud and excited. I've never really had an action figure before, so for her to be a *Star Wars* character is amazing!

Can you talk about Sabine's relationship to the other characters?
Hera's the matriarch of the whole group; she takes care of everyone, which is funny because Vanessa's a bit like that.

It's like art imitates life, or life imitates art,

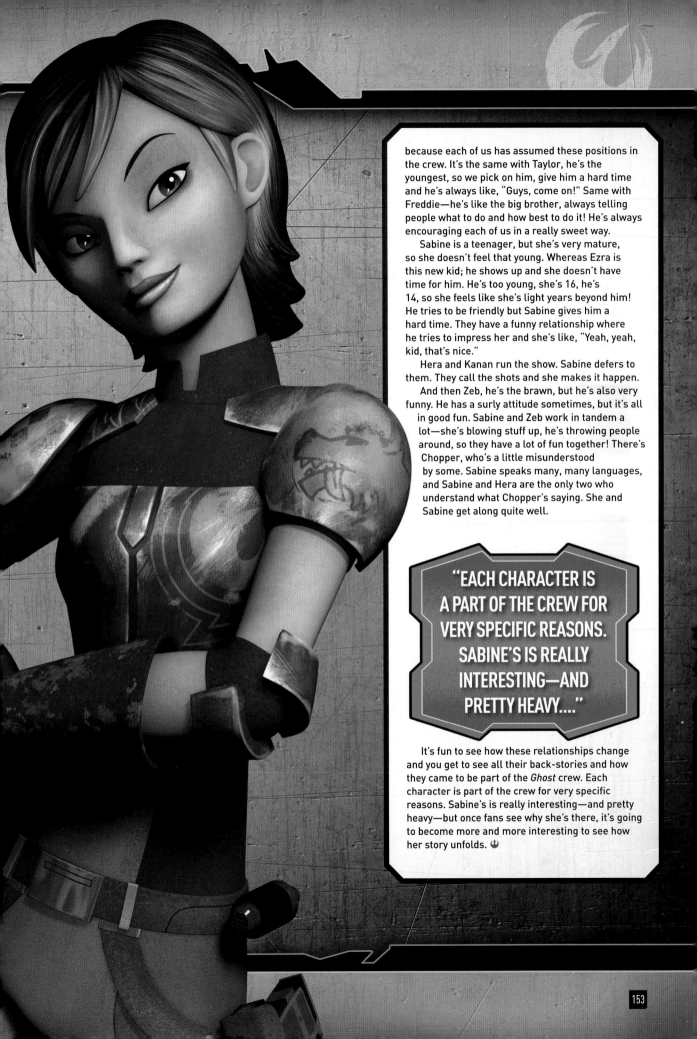

because each of us has assumed these positions in the crew. It's the same with Taylor, he's the youngest, so we pick on him, give him a hard time and he's always like, "Guys, come on!" Same with Freddie—he's like the big brother, always telling people what to do and how best to do it! He's always encouraging each of us in a really sweet way.

Sabine is a teenager, but she's very mature, so she doesn't feel that young. Whereas Ezra is this new kid; he shows up and she doesn't have time for him. He's too young, she's 16, he's 14, so she feels like she's light years beyond him! He tries to be friendly but Sabine gives him a hard time. They have a funny relationship where he tries to impress her and she's like, "Yeah, yeah, kid, that's nice."

Hera and Kanan run the show. Sabine defers to them. They call the shots and she makes it happen.

And then Zeb, he's the brawn, but he's also very funny. He has a surly attitude sometimes, but it's all in good fun. Sabine and Zeb work in tandem a lot—she's blowing stuff up, he's throwing people around, so they have a lot of fun together! There's Chopper, who's a little misunderstood by some. Sabine speaks many, many languages, and Sabine and Hera are the only two who understand what Chopper's saying. She and Sabine get along quite well.

> "EACH CHARACTER IS A PART OF THE CREW FOR VERY SPECIFIC REASONS. SABINE'S IS REALLY INTERESTING—AND PRETTY HEAVY...."

It's fun to see how these relationships change and you get to see all their back-stories and how they came to be part of the *Ghost* crew. Each character is part of the crew for very specific reasons. Sabine's is really interesting—and pretty heavy—but once fans see why she's there, it's going to become more and more interesting to see how her story unfolds. ☻

100 PAGES!

STAR WARS
INSIDER

EXCLUSIVE
Jar Jar Binks:
The Real Story!

PHANTOM FACTS!
Discover the Secrets of
The Phantom Menace

FLIGHT CLUB!
Actor Ralph Brown
Takes the Controls

**SITH VERSUS
SEPARATIST**
Maul Takes on Dooku

THE SAGA BEGINS

CELEBRATE 10 YEARS OF STAR WARS:
EPISODE I THE PHANTOM MENACE

ISSUE #109
May/June 2009 $7.99

MORE MAUL!
The Expanded
Universe of Episode I

BLASTER!
Books, Collecting, Toys,
Classic Scene, Ask Lobot,
Comics, Bounty Hunters,
Bantha Tracks and More!

7 25274 22493 7

ROB COLEMAN
VISUAL EFFECTS

ISSUE 109
MAY/JUNE 2009

When I had previously interviewed Rob Coleman about his work on *Star Wars: The Clone Wars*, I'd casually asked if would be interested in being interviewed about his work on *Star Wars: The Phantom Menace*, for inclusion in our 10th anniversary tribute issue. He paused, giving me cause to wonder if perhaps he didn't want to discuss his groundbreaking effects work on the movie. "10 years?" he asked. "Wow. I had no idea. Has it really been that long?"

Of course, Coleman started work on the film some time before 1999, such was the massive undertaking on such a landmark project. And, once he got over the shock of how much time had passed, he was happy to share tales of his experience making the film—working with George Lucas to realize his vision with some of the most striking images in the entire saga.—**Jonathan Wilkins**

Rob Coleman (born April 27, 1964) is a two-time Oscar nominee for his animation work on Star Wars: The Phantom Menace *and* Star Wars: Attack of the Clones. *He was nominated for two BAFTA Awards for his work on* Men in Black *and* Star Wars: The Phantom Menace.

THIS MONTH, FAR, FAR AWAY....

Star Wars: The Clone Wars: The Gauntlet of Death released as part of Free Comic Book Day

Star Wars: The Clone Wars 6: Slaves of the Republic - Chapter 6: Escape from Kadavo released

Star Wars: The Clone Wars: No Prisoners released

Star Wars: Vector Volume 2, Chapters 3 & 4 released

Star Wars: Knights of the Old Republic 41: Dueling Ambitions, Part 3 released

Darth Vader makes a cameo appearance in *Night at the Museum: Battle of the Smithsonian*

Star Wars: The Clone Wars: The Wind Raiders of Taloraan released

Star Wars: Legacy 36: Renegade released

Star Wars: Knights of the Old Republic 42: Masks released

Star Wars: Fate of the Jedi: Omen released

Star Wars: Legacy 37: Tatooine, Part 1 released

Star Wars: Agents of Deception, the fourth card set of the Galaxies Trading Card Game released

Star Wars: The Clone Wars: The Downfall of a Droid and *Destroy Malevolence* storybooks released

CHARACTER BUILDING

ROB COLEMAN'S ROLE AS ANIMATION DIRECTOR ON *STAR WARS*: EPISODE I *THE PHANTOM MENACE* SAW HIM RESPONSIBLE FOR THE WEIRD AND WONDERFUL CREATURES THAT POPULATED THE MOVIE. IT WAS A CHALLENGE THAT PROVED NEARLY IMPOSSIBLE.

WORDS: JONATHAN WILKINS

Star Wars Insider: When you joined Industrial Light & Magic in 1993 were you hoping to work on the new Star Wars trilogy?

Rob Coleman: Actually, no. Even though we'd heard about George Lucas talking about another trilogy when the first one came out, a new movie was not on my mind when I joined ILM. Around 1996 he came by for an assembly in the main theater, and he shared with us that he was going to start writing the second trilogy. I remember sitting at the back of the theater thinking, "Whoah! That's pretty cool!" I didn't decide then that I wanted to go for that job. When *Men In Black* came out in 1997, I heard through Jim Morris [head of ILM at that time] that George really liked my work on that. I found out that they wanted me to fly over to London because they were in pre-production at Leavesden, and they were considering me to be the animation director on the new Star Wars movie.

Was it a daunting project to be involved in?

I was asked to spend 10 days with George—it was a 10-day interview. Even though I was working for his company ILM, I had to demonstrate to Rick [McCallum, producer] and George that I was the right person for the job, and that involved speaking when I was spoken to, answering questions articulately enough, and showing that I had a personality that matched George's. I ended up ticking all those boxes. I found it very easy to be with George. I was terrified more about the job than of him, because it had dawned on me that I remembered what it was like to be 19 and wanting to see another *Star Wars* movie. I recall coming back after I'd been told that I had the job and the insomnia started. I was thinking about everyone on the planet who's been waiting for a *Star Wars* movie, and now I'm the animation director.

I remember for a couple of months not really sleeping very well and it was way worse than butterflies in the stomach—it was full-on panic! I remember getting to a point where I actually went to George and told him about the pressure of the world waiting for this movie. He said, "What are you talking about? You have one person to make happy—me! If you make me happy, it's on my shoulders." He added, "I'm happy. Everything you're doing is great, so just calm down." I went home and slept like a baby!

What does an animation director do?

The animation director is responsible for supervising all of the digital characters in the film. I represented a team of actors that were bringing the digital characters, like Jar Jar, Watto, and Sebulba, to life. George would present a scene to me, for example Watto's junkyard—which

was the first sequence we did for the film—and he would talk me through what he wanted. He had filmed the rehearsal of Andy Secombe [the voice of Watto], so I could see his facial expressions and body motion. He turned the scene over to me and then it was my responsibility to pull one cohesive performance out of a team of five or 10 animators who were working on the character of Watto. It was also my responsibility to present that work to George as a work in progress, moving towards a final version and its inclusion in the film.

Can you recall your initial thoughts on seeing the script—did it seem achievable at that time?
Not at all! Once we came back from the shoot, we then went into production at ILM. Chrissie England, who was producing for us, would have Wednesday lunchtime supervisors meetings with myself, Dennis Muren, John Knoll, and John Squires. There was a single line on the discussion: "Can we get the movie done?" For six months the answer was "No." Any way we looked at it, either mathematically, from a staffing point of view, or from a rendering and computing point of view there was no way we were going to be able to get the movie done, so there was an undercurrent of panic. This movie was 10 times bigger than the previous biggest film we had just done,

Men In Black, which had 200 shots and this thing had 2,000 shots! It was an enormous jump up for us from a logistics point of view, so when we saw the script we spent months breaking it down into its component parts—what are the assets, what are the environments, what are the technical challenges, and how are we going to do certain scenes? John Knoll would break the scenes down and say "We're going to do these as miniatures, and these are going to be computer graphics." Dennis Muren, who was working on the Gungan battle, did the Naboo scenes out on the plains and Scott Squires did the city scenes. Each supervisor had his own concerns. I was running between the three units, because George and Rick wanted to ensure that the performances were consistent across all three groups.

Did you get a sense of the work becoming easier as you found your way?
It was an uphill battle for the entire show because we were breaking every software tool and hardware restriction we had at ILM. We were challenging the facility and the people in it to the absolute max and beyond. You watch people running marathons, and they cross the line and fall over—that's what it felt like to do *The Phantom Menace*. On *Attack of the Clones* I ran across the finish line and I still had air in my lungs, and on *Revenge of the Sith*

I didn't break a sweat! That's because we developed a greater understanding of what George wanted, and the technology was much more robust. That's the real strength of ILM. You are surrounded by true geniuses and everyone is pulling together; that's how we were able to do it.

Are there things you did on *Revenge of the Sith* that you couldn't have achieved on *The Phantom Menace*?
Oh yes, tons. For example, there was an early discussion on whether Yoda was going to be digital in *The Phantom Menace*. I was willing to take it on, but I was really concerned at the acting ability of my animators and whether the simulator could do the cloth rendering. I was very happy on each film with what we achieved at that moment in time. We were maxing out everything and there was nothing more we could've put in there in terms of fidelity or subtly in the facial performances.

A lot of fans would like to see the digital Yoda in *The Phantom Menace*.
George certainly goes back to his films and tinkers with them, so it's a possibility. Maybe one day!

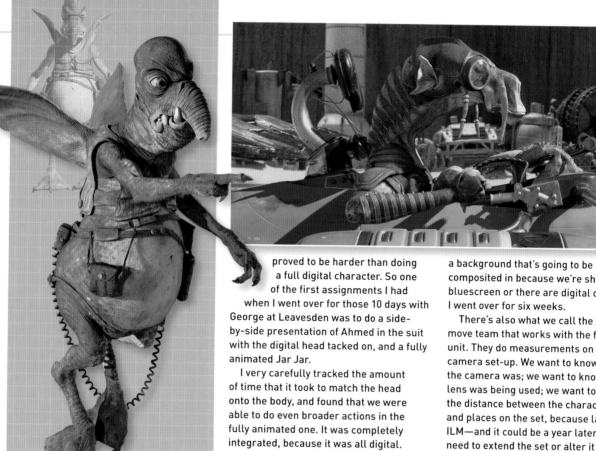

proved to be harder than doing a full digital character. So one of the first assignments I had when I went over for those 10 days with George at Leavesden was to do a side-by-side presentation of Ahmed in the suit with the digital head tacked on, and a fully animated Jar Jar.

I very carefully tracked the amount of time that it took to match the head onto the body, and found that we were able to do even broader actions in the fully animated one. It was completely integrated, because it was all digital. George noticed that right away. We still kept Ahmed in the suit for lighting reference, but he was fully animated for all the shots.

Was there a lot to do on set for ILM?
There was actually a mini-crew on set. John Knoll was there every day, because on a *Star Wars* film every shot has some element of visual effects, whether it be

a background that's going to be composited in because we're shooting over bluescreen or there are digital characters. I went over for six weeks.

There's also what we call the match-move team that works with the first unit. They do measurements on every camera set-up. We want to know where the camera was; we want to know what lens was being used; we want to know the distance between the characters and places on the set, because later at ILM—and it could be a year later—we may need to extend the set or alter it because of George's desire to make changes from when we first shot it.

The match-move team measures lights, and the position of the lights. We have a sphere that is matte gray on one side and silver on the other. If we shoot the gray side it shows you where the key light and the fill light are coming from, and if you swing the ball around, it reflects the entire set into the ball. You can unwrap the set

Jar Jar was certainly a groundbreaking achievement in cinema history.
George always said that he was for the younger fans, and he nailed it. I was given the responsibility of bringing the character to life and when Jar Jar got panned, I took it hard. I flew back from the New York premiere with George and he asked how I was feeling. I said, "Everybody hates Jar Jar." He replied, "Not everybody hates Jar Jar; the kids love Jar Jar, and you'll see that. The other thing is that they're responding to him like he's a real character on screen. They're having a visceral reaction to him the same way that people responded to Chris Tucker's character in *The Fifth Element*. You should be happy that your work is being seen as an actor. You got over a high bar that no one's giving you any credit for right now, and [your achievement is] significant."

What challenges were involved in making the character work?
The initial thought was that it was going to be Ahmed Best's body with a digital head on top. Ahmed had a full suit from the neck down, and then he wore a Jar Jar head on top of his head, so the live actors had the correct eyeline. He performed everything for us, so the costume ended up being a fantastic lighting reference for John Knoll's team. Adding the head

out of the silver ball, and then triangulate where all the lights and cameras are. They got notebooks filled with measurements and positions, and they worked with continuity as well, so they knew which shots George favored.

How did the actors deal with all this?
Liam Neeson was very interested in how they were going to move, and what they were going to look like. He was very tuned in to what the imaginary was going to be.

Natalie Portman came up to me at the New York premiere and said, "I know I was there, but I had no idea that it was going to look like it looked!" She was swept along by the whole process.

They were very cooperative, but I think they thought it was a little crazy, too! Ewan McGregor just shook his head, because I'd go up with my laptop to show him what the scene was going to look like, and he'd say, "Yep, alright, just tell me where I'm looking, who's coming at me, and what do they look like?"

How did the battle droids' distinctive animation come about?
It came about by mistake. We had some motion, and we put it on a battle droid model, but it hadn't tracked properly and the butt ended up sticking out more than we would have liked. George saw it and liked it. It made them look more goofy. To George, the battle droids were very much a work in progress in terms of evolving from a battle droid to the super battle droids we see in the later movies. He told us, "These things are just being cranked out; they're not very smart." Their heads are always moving around and they don't quite know what's going on.

Did Watto present a different challenge?
Well he did, just because of his design—he's got that huge belly! I remember some people at ILM saying because of his wing ratio he'd never fly. I happened to be watching one of the science and nature channels and there was a documentary on bumblebees and a scientist said, "Actually the wing to body ratio is quite confusing, because technically they shouldn't be able to fly." I went back in and said, "The bumblebee has wings that are too small, so Watto's got wings that are too small. And by the way, his belly's filled with helium!"

How did you come up with Sebulba's walking style?
That came from the lead animator for the character, Miguel Fuertez. He had seen a 1932 film called Freaks; in that movie there's a man with no legs, Johnny Eck, and he walks on his hands. He was the true inspiration for Sebulba's walk. Miguel and another animator, Patrick Bueno, pretty much handled everything for Sebulba.

I loved how he played with his whiskers, when they were standing beside the Podracer. The great thing about being an animation director is that you can present the scenes to the animators and they will improvise. It came out just like a real actor would take on the character: Where's the character in the story? Where is he going? Where has he been? What's his attitude? What does he think about this boy? He ended up being like [cartoon archvillain] Snidely Whiplash!

Is there anything in the movie that you really wanted to do that couldn't be done at the time?
We pretty well achieved everything that George asked us to do. There was one sentence in the script that took six months to deal with. And that sentence was something like: The Gungan army marches out to battle. Prior to that, ILM didn't have a way to handle that many characters on the screen at the same time. When I went to the premiere my wife had to get up and go to the bathroom and missed that scene. When she came back she asked, "Did I miss anything?" I said, "Yeah, six months of my life!" I remember being really worried that we would never be able to deliver those huge, epic shots of the Gungans

because the software team, although it was working as hard as it could, took a lot longer than originally projected. The months were going by and we were only just able to achieve that shot!

How important is it to incorporate the actual actor into the character design?
If you look at some of the great Disney films, the characters look like the voice actors. For example, Terry-Thomas playing King John in *Robin Hood* or George Sanders doing the voice of Shere Khan in *The Jungle Book*, have a resemblance to the actors. As an animator, if your character looks like the voice actor, you are able to grab facial expressions that are particular to that person. For example, Brian Blessed's large jowls when he shakes his face around as Boss Nass were added to our animation. I always had George film the actors, so we were able to actually look at Brian's mouth and his jowls. They are a significant part of his personality and his facial expressions. You can ask the animator to match it.

What is your proudest achievement?
To have led an incredible group of animators and to have produced high quality work that I am very proud of. ☻

THE FIRST ORDER COLLECTORS' COVER
CHOOSE YOUR SIDE: ARE YOU WITH THE FIRST ORDER OR THE RESISTANCE?

STAR WARS

THE FORCE AWAKENS

INSIDER

FEATURING

HARRISON FORD
CARRIE FISHER
ANTHONY DANIELS
PETER MAYHEW
DAISY RIDLEY
OSCAR ISAAC
JOHN BOYEGA
LUPITA NYONG'O
ADAM DRIVER
GWENDOLINE CHRISTIE
DOMHNALL GLEESON
J.J. ABRAMS
AND MORE!

ISSUE #162
US $7.99
CAN $9.99
JAN 2016

TITAN

BB-8
DROID APPRECIATION!

ISSUE 162
JANUARY 2016

THIS MONTH, FAR, FAR AWAY....

Star Wars: Lando trade paperback released

Star Wars 15: From the Journals of Old Ben Kenobi released

Star Wars Rebels "A Princess on Lothal," and "The Protector of Concord Dawn" aired on Disney XD

Star Wars Volume 2: Showdown on the Smuggler's Moon trade paperback released

Star Wars: Kanan 10: First Blood, Part IV: The Mesas of Mygeeto released

I vividly remember where I was when I was blown away by *Star Wars* newest star. Celebration Anaheim in 2015 was filled with anticipation for *Star Wars: The Force Awakens*. There was a sense of excitement in the air, mainly centered around the screening of the trailer and the panel featuring the stars of the movie.

But it was game over when BB-8 rolled onto the stage. There he was: an instantly iconic character who felt new, yet as familiar as an old friend. As he rolled around the stage, I started to wonder how he worked, and then stopped. I didn't want to know. I just wanted to believe.—**Jonathan Wilkins**

WATCH OUT! BB-8 IS ABOUT!

THE CAST AND CREW OF *STAR WARS: THE FORCE AWAKENS* ON WORKING WITH THE SAGA'S NEWEST ICON!

JOHN BOYEGA

"BB-8 is amazing. BB-8 is so cute and charismatic... and a little bit feisty. I'm starting to wonder if R2-D2 is a distant cousin. BB-8 is lovely to work with. I have to talk about BB-8 as an actor, because BB-8 is actually there on set. It's puppetry; it's animatronics, and BB-8 is a combination of both. It's been amazing working with BB-8. Sometimes he's rude and has to work on his attitude a bit. But, as a droid that just got this part, he has a long way to go..."

OSCAR ISAAC

"His design is amazing. I believe J.J. Abrams actually came up with the design, which is so ingenious, because it feels like I've seen it before. It feels like it's familiar to the *Star Wars* universe, but it's not; It's completely new. The fact that it's a ball that moves around, it looks like he has a little belly; it's very cute, but he's so expressive because of that, and has so much more room for expression. He really comes to life, and they have so many different versions of him. They have a puppeteer who's in a blue suit or green suit, and there's one by himself that's remote controlled, and there's a stationary one."

ANTHONY DANIELS

"One of the really great things, and it took me totally by surprise, was BB-8. I was on the set, and I'm watching this droid coming to life in front of me in motion capture. I'm only a few feet away and there's a guy dressed entirely in green, acting. But I still couldn't understand how BB-8 functions. I was instantly enchanted. Then we move on and now I'm in a scene with BB-8. You'd expect me to say BB-8 is in a scene with a star it's like I'm in a scene with him. He's the most delightful character. Sorry, R2, eat your heart out. I think people are going to fall in love with BB-8. There's something there. There are many creatures on this set, particularly since this is such a diverse universe. There are creatures of every shape and weirdness, and mechanics. There are humanoid aliens of every single color and shape and quality. The diversity will help people to dive into it, because there's something there for everybody. But I think BB-8 will get all the [great] reviews. Anyone acting in a scene with BB-8 should watch out!"

DAISY RIDLEY

"Meeting BB-8 was tricky, because I hadn't worked with a person on screen, let alone a little droid. It was so tricky at first, but it made acting with other characters easier much later on."

BB-8: DROID SECRETS REVEALED!

THE OFFICIAL MAGAZINE OF THE *STAR WARS* SAGA

STAR WARS

INSIDER

ART OF WARS!

See the Art that Helped Bring *STAR WARS: THE FORCE AWAKENS* to the Big Screen!

OBI-WAN KENOBI Why the FORCE is with Him!

EXCLUSIVE!

35 YEARS OF THE *STAR WARS* **RADIO DRAMA!**

Director and Producer Interviews, Inside!

ISSUE #163
FEB/MAR 2016
US $7.99
CAN $9.99
TITAN

SIMON PEGG
UNKAR PLUTT

THIS MONTH, FAR, FAR AWAY....

Star Wars: Rolling with BB-8! released

Star Wars: Obi-Wan & Anakin, Part II released

Star Wars Rebels "Legends of the Lasat," "The Call," "Shroud of Darkness," and "The Forgotten Droid" aired on Disney XD

Alethea McGrath, (Jocasta Nu), dies, aged 95

Star Wars: Darth Vader 16: The Shu-Torun War, Part I released

Drewe Henley (Red Leader in *A New Hope*), dies, aged 76

Star Wars: The Force Awakens: A Junior Novel released in print

Star Wars: The Original Trilogy: A Graphic Novel released

Star Wars: Darth Vader 17: The Shu-Torun War, Part II released

Star Wars: Chewbacca trade paperback released

Star Wars Galaxy: The Original Topps Trading Card Series released

Star Wars: Kanan 12: First Blood, Epilogue: The Ties That Bind released

Simon Pegg has made no secret of his love of *Star Wars*, and a new *Star Wars* movie directed by frequent collaborator J.J. Abrams made it seem that a cameo of some sort was on the cards. That was eventually confirmed in a behind-the-scenes promotional video.

I have to confess, I didn't notice he was even in the film first time around, so complete was his performance under prosthetics and a generously proportioned fat-suit!—**Jonathan Wilkins**

Simon John Pegg (born February 14, 1970) is an actor, comedian, screenwriter, and producer. He is best known for co-writing and starring in Shaun of the Dead *(2004),* Hot Fuzz *(2007), and* The World's End *(2013), and the TV series* Spaced *(1999–2001). He also plays Scotty in the rebooted* Star Trek *(2009),* Star Trek Into Darkness *(2013), and* Star Trek Beyond *(2016).*

SIMON PEGG ON BEING A
LIFELONG *STAR WARS* FAN
AND PLAYING UNKAR PLUTT
IN *STAR WARS: THE
FORCE AWAKENS*!

FROM FAN TO FAR, FAR AWAY!

ON GETTING THE ROLE OF UNKAR PLUTT...

I've done five films with J.J. Abrams; one with him as a producer. When I heard he was doing *Star Wars*, I was immediately on the phone to him, because as a *Star Trek* alumnus, I was kind of concerned with what was going to happen. I thought maybe I could be a voice or something because being in it as me with my face would be a little too meta. I imagine people would think, *Oh, it's him from Star Trek*, and my own conscience was saying that might spoil it. Then we discussed the idea of me playing a character that was in full prosthetic makeup, which meant I could have my space cake and eat it.

ON A LIFELONG LOVE OF *STAR WARS*...

It starts about 37 years ago for me when I first saw *Star Wars*; it pretty much changed my life completely. It shaped my childhood in terms of what I was interested in and engendered the love of film that I have, and my career is a result of that. So really I have to thank *Star Wars* for putting me here in a way, because it's what fueled my imagination and got me interested in this business.

ON SUITING UP FOR *STAR WARS*...

We did all the close-up work at Pinewood because the mask had to be glued to my face, so the articulation was there. We couldn't do that in Abu Dhabi because of the heat, so we used the pull-over mask, which is nevertheless still as much rubber. Then there's sort of a fat suit and rubber gloves. It was extremely hot and worryingly, at times, claustrophobic. My heart rate would go up a little bit and I would just have to keep going, "It's *Star Wars*! It's *Star Wars*!" But this is what you do. You get into ridiculous outfits and makeups and you suffer because it's so much better if it's real, if you're there, and if it's a genuine thing that is interacting with actors, not just a digital creation. So I was prepared to suffer without complaint as I melted inside this silicone prison!

ON BEING AN ON-SET STAR WARS EXPERT...

It's funny having conversations with people about what-happened-when because I'm pretty good with my Star Wars knowledge. Every now and again, I'll get asked about something and I'm able to go, "Well, actually, I think you'll find in The Empire Strikes Back that..." It's a place where you can just wield that nerdiness with pride.

ON BEING IMPRESSED BY THE CREATURES...

I love the fact that they got in some of the guys from War Horse to do some of the puppeteering. Physical must never be let go of. CG is a wonderful tool but it has its place; it shouldn't do everything. Once it starts doing everything, the film will become a cartoon. Whereas if you use real stuff that actors can interact with and be there with, there's a feeling of proximity and jeopardy that you cannot achieve with CG entirely. So it's wonderful to see all this stuff being made.

Neal Scanlan, the creature effects supervisor, is extraordinary. I remember when we were out in Abu Dhabi and they built this little thing that comes out of the sand and looks like a classic Star Wars creature. It's on a sort of hydraulic and then it goes back down, and I just remember thinking, these guys are having a blast on this. I would bet that the vast majority of people working on this in physical effects were inspired by Star Wars.

ON THE CRUCIAL ELEMENTS...

The main part of J.J.'s mission statement about making these movies was to continue what the first three films set up. This film is the sequel to Return of the Jedi, obviously. The prequels happened before the first three films in terms of the chronology. So this film has to feel like an extension of Episode VI. To do that, J.J. has gone to great lengths in terms of how he's shooting the movie, in terms of shooting on film, the music, andthe design. He wants it to feel like part of

that universe, part of that series, and not something separate. Being part of it, you feel that straight away. You know what this is and I think when you watch the movies they will feel very much like Star Wars. You will see that in the physical effects element, the practical sets, the makeups and the masks. All these things are present and that makes a huge difference. When you see computer-generated stuff, if it's obviously computer-generated, it stops you from thinking about how they did it because you have an abstract idea of how they do that. Someone does this in a room and then that appears. That is somehow less awe-inspiring and less impressive than seeing a real, full-size Millennium Falcon sitting in a forest. I think that's what J.J. completely gets in terms of what makes Star Wars amazing.

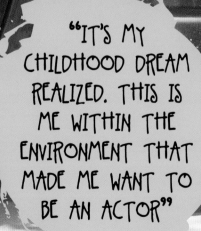

"IT'S MY CHILDHOOD DREAM REALIZED. THIS IS ME WITHIN THE ENVIRONMENT THAT MADE ME WANT TO BE AN ACTOR"

ON DIRECTOR J.J. ABRAMS...

J.J.'s from the right generation. He's a man who was inspired by it and who grew up on it. Like me, he was the right age when it came out; we were its absolute target audience. He understands it fully. He understands it as a fan as well as a creative. He's just absolutely the right man for the job. As well as that, you have someone who, on set, is a complete delight to work with. He's very, very keen. His sets are happy, productive places where everybody is inspired and active and involved, and he does that by leading from the head down. J.J. sets an incredible example on set. You're always in no doubt that this is a fun place, but it's a place of hard work, and that's really important when you're filmmaking. It should never be too serious; it should never be arduous and it should never be easy. J.J. totally has exactly the right approach to filmmaking and that's what's needed to make this film.

ON A DREAM COME TRUE...

There's not a register that it can possibly be measured on. It's my childhood dream realized. This is me within the environment that made me want to be a film actor. It doesn't get any cooler than that. To be able to hug Chewie and lean on R2-D2, and talk to Carrie Fisher and Mark Hamill—these are the things that I dreamt of as a kid. I use to fantasize about getting to do that stuff and here I am doing it. It's not lost on

THE ESSENTIAL *STAR WARS: THE FORCE AWAKENS* COLLECTIBLES!

THE JEDI REVEALED: SECRETS OF THE FORCE EXPLORED

STAR WARS

INSIDER

START WARS!

TAKE ARMS!
TAKE AIM!
TAKE NO PRISONERS!

STAR WARS
BATTLEFRONT
EA

IS HERE!

PLUS:
AN EXCLUSIVE
TIE-IN STORY!

ISSUE #161
US $7.99
CAN $9.99
NOV/DEC 2015
TITAN

JORDAN D. WHITE
MARVEL STAR WARS

ISSUE 161
NOVEMBER/DECEMBER 2015

Jordan D. White's editorship of Marvel's *Star Wars* comics has been a triumph. The assorted ongoing titles, miniseries, and one-off stories have been well received by fans and critics.

A genuinely fascinating character, he was at *Star Wars* Celebration when I met him—proudly brandishing a poster featuring C-3PO and R2-D2 encouraging kids to get immunized, and talking about his fondness for playing John Williams' epic *Star Wars* themes on a ukulele. I knew straight away that he would be an ideal subject for *Insider*'s regular *My Star Wars* column.— **Jonathan Wilkins**

Jordan D. White has overseen the Star Wars *comics line since 2015. He is also the editor of Marvel's* X-Men *and* Deadpool *books, including Jason Aaron and Kieron Gillen's concurrent* Wolverine and the X-Men *and* Uncanny X-Men *series. He edited the* Hulk *and* Hercules *lines from 2008 to 2011.*

THIS MONTH, FAR, FAR AWAY....

Star Wars: AT-AT Attack! released

Star Wars: Droid Factory released

LEGO Star Wars: Small Scenes from a Big Galaxy released

Star Wars: Battlefront: Twilight Company released

Star Wars Legends Epic Collection: The Empire Volume 2 released

Star Wars: Princess Leia trade paperback released

Star Wars: Kanan Volume 1: The Last Padawan trade paperback released

Star Wars 11: Showdown on the Smuggler's Moon, Part IV released

Star Wars Rebels "Brothers of the Broken Horn" aired on Disney XD

*Star Wars: **Darth Vader 12**: Shadows and Secrets, Part VI* released

Star Wars: Chewbacca, Part III released

Star Wars: The Force Awakens premieres in Los Angeles, California

Star Wars: Darth Vader Annual 1 released

Star Wars: Kanan 9: First Blood, Part III: The Canyons of Kardoa released

Star Wars: The Force Awakens novelization eBook released

Star Wars: The Force Awakens released

UNDER JORDAN D. WHITE'S EDITORSHIP, THE *STAR WARS* MARVEL COMICS LINE CONTINUES TO THRIVE. *INSIDER* MET WITH THE MARVEL MASTERMIND TO DISCUSS HIS EARLY MEMORIES OF THE SAGA, AND PLAYING JOHN WILLIAMS' CLASSICS ON HIS UKULELE! INTERVIEW BY MARK NEWBOLD

Can you remember when you saw *Star Wars* for the first time?
I can't. I was born on December 18, 1979, so I was too young to see either *Star Wars* or *The Empire Strikes Back* in the theaters. *Return of the Jedi* was one of the first movies my parents ever took me to see at the young age of three. But there were VHS copies of the films taped off HBO from as early as I can remember, and I watched them over and over again. Many of the earliest stories my family has of me are *Star Wars*-related—like me theorizing the droids are neither good nor evil, as they are programmed how to behave.

What first grabbed you about the saga?
Honestly, since I always remember it being part of my life, I cannot say for

certain. I assume, though, that it was because the saga just has such a great, straightforward, heroic arc. It's so easy to get caught up in Luke's quest. I see people make fun of Luke as a naïve farmboy sometimes... but that's part of why he's such a great surrogate for us all to take our first steps into this larger world.

When did you first become aware of *Star Wars* fandom?
I don't think I was aware of "fandom" as a child, other than that I, and all my friends, dug the movies and toys. The first time I remember being aware of the extra distance *Star Wars* fans will go was in the early days of the internet. I remember a video called *Quentin Tarantino's Star Wars* that someone

made with toys. And, of course, [1997 fan-made spoof film] *Troops*. I still listen to *Star Wars: The Musical* from www.infauxmedia.com on a regular basis. I love all the amazing fan-made art that *Star Wars* inspires.

Did you read the original Marvel run back in the day?
I didn't. I am not sure why exactly. The run ended when I was seven. I guess I might have bought a couple issues and just forgot about them. I was more into *Spider-Man* in my early comic-book reading years. I didn't branch out into buying more non-Spidey books until the early 1990s, at which point the Marvel run was over. I'd like to, now... but there is a lot of in-canon stuff to keep up with.